Self-Care
for
Caregivers

What readers say about
Self-Care for Caregivers: A Twelve Step Approach

REV. PAUL KELLER, caregiver and author of *Living in the Promises*
"Once I started reading *Self-Care for Caregivers,* I could not put it down. It seems impossible to overstate the potential value of this book."

DEBORAH HARMON-PUGH, SPHR, editor of *The Healthy Caregiver*
"The ultimate goal of caregiving is achieving secure and fulfilling lifestyles for all members of the care relationship. This book is an outstanding guide to managing the complex realities of caregiving."

GAIL R. MITCHELL, *Empowering Caregivers*
"This is a remarkable guide for all caregivers. The exercises are geared towards gaining insight into your 'inner self.'"

CHARLES BENTZ, husband of Alzheimer's patient
"The way this book grasps the multi-faceted problem of Alzheimer caregiving is remarkable. It offers caregivers insight and support to properly, wisely care for themselves as they care for their loved one."

VICKI L. SCHMALL, PH.D., retired gerontology specialist, University of Oregon
"This book gives caregivers a framework for making tough decisions without being consumed by resentment, guilt, or regret . . . for setting boundaries in caregiving and saying no without feeling guilty."

ROBERT WATSON, husband of woman with multiple sclerosis
"Whether you're new to the Twelve Step philosophy or a firm believer in it, you'll find here a way to survive and succeed in one of life's most difficult roles—that of a caregiver."

Self-Care *for* Caregivers

A Twelve Step Approach

PAT SAMPLES

DIANE LARSEN
MARVIN LARSEN

HAZELDEN

Hazelden
Center City, Minnesota 55012-0176

1-800-328-0094
1-651-213-4590 (Fax)
www.hazelden.org

Library of Congress Cataloging-in-Publication Data

Samples, Pat.
  Self-care for caregivers : a twelve step approach / Pat Samples, Diane Larsen, Marvin Larsen.
    p. cm.
  Originally published: 1991.
  Includes bibliographical references.
  ISBN 1-56838-560-9
    1. Twelve-step programs—Religious aspects—Meditations. 2. Caregivers—Religious
life. I. Larsen, Diane. II. Larsen, Marvin. III. Title.

BL624.5 .S25 2000
362.1—dc21

                                                          00-044880

Editor's Note:

Hazelden Information and Educational Services offers a variety of information on chemical dependency and related areas. Our publications do not necessarily represent Hazelden programs, nor do they officially speak for any Twelve Step organization.

Permission to reprint the Twelve Steps does not mean that Alcoholics Anonymous has reviewed or approved the contents of this publication, nor that AA agrees with the views expressed herein. AA is a program of recovery from alcoholism only. Use of the Twelve Steps in connection with programs which are patterned after AA but which address other problems does not imply otherwise.

CONTENTS

Preface

People often ask me if I wrote this book because of being a caregiver myself. In part, that's true. I've been a caregiver at times for several people close to me and I wanted to share with others some of the strength and hope that the Twelve Steps have given me in those situations.

In addition, I've been deeply moved by the stories I've heard from my friends Marvin and Diane Larsen and from other caregivers. I've been touched by their pain and wisdom. I've felt a kinship with them. That sense of kinship, of knowing I'm not alone, is at the heart of the Twelve Step program. It has brought me great comfort over the years. It has also stirred in me a desire to enlarge the circle of kinship so that other caregivers may experience the benefits of the program.

I've been involved in Twelve Step programs for over fifteen years. I've been caring about caregivers for almost a decade. That special desire to be of service to caregivers has become my personal mission. I have given many talks and workshops to caregivers and to the professionals who work with them, sharing the message of hope and inviting them to turn inward to find peace of mind. I believe that we all have within us the wisdom we need to make sane and healthy choices for ourselves in the midst of the challenges of caregiving. But if we don't take care of ourselves, it can be harder for us to tap into that wisdom. The Twelve Step program shows us how to take care of ourselves so we can maintain and deepen our serenity.

I have been pleased to see the results of sharing this good news. Many people have called me to tell me how much the book helped them and to ask for a second copy to pass along to a struggling friend or relative. I remember one woman, whose husband had Alzheimer's, telling me she kept a copy of the book under her pillow. That way, when her husband would wake up and wander during the night, she could reach for it and find solace. Another caregiver, deep in depression when she first came across the book, expressed tearful gratitude for showing her a way out.

I have also been gratified by the responses of professional caregivers who have told me that they too have benefited from the Twelve Step approach described in this book. Nurses, social workers, hospice workers, and other medical, social service, and religious professionals tend to know burnout all too well. I remember speaking to a group of clergy, inviting them to send caregivers from their congregation to a Self-Care for Caregivers workshop I was conducting. One of them asked if they (the clergy members) could come too. Then they began telling me their stories of the burden of having to care for their own parents and family members on top of their ministerial duties. Even these clerics with strong religious foundations were glad to be reminded of the need to rely on a Power greater than themselves.

A nursing director at a mental hospital told me she turned to the book often when the many legal and administrative demands on her, plus her patients' complex needs, were pushing her to the edge of rage and tears. She said she was learning to step back from overcaring and to ask for what she needed.

You may find many ways to get the most out of this book. One good way is to find another caregiver, or several, to share it with. Meet together or talk on the phone regularly. Discuss each step and how you are using the step to help you. Talk about the exercises described at the end of each step and what you have learned from doing them. Focus on supporting each other's growth and progress.

You might consider organizing a Caregivers Anonymous group. A few of these groups have started in recent years.

However, there is no formal structure in place to support them, at least not at the time this book went to press. You can contact other Twelve Step groups such as Alcoholics Anonymous or Al-Anon to gather ideas about how to run a group meeting and to learn more about other Twelve Step resources. Hazelden also provides many resources that you may find helpful.

If you are a medical, religious, or social service professional, you may wish to help the family caregivers you know obtain copies of this book. One organization bought thousands of copies to give out to the caregivers they serve. An adult day care center used the book as a discussion guide for an on-going caregiver support group they sponsored. Other organizations have sponsored talks and workshops based on the book. You may find your own way of using the book both for your own needs and for the caregivers that turn to you for support.

My main hope is that you will use this book to help you take care of yourself, and in so doing, find for yourself greater peace of mind.

Pat Samples

Introduction

Taking care of others has been a big part of our entire married life of twenty-eight years. We have raised our own three children and over the years, a number of their friends have lived with us for periods of time. Any time someone we knew needed a place to stay or a little looking after, we were quick to offer our love and our home. Once, for a time, we took in a cousin's fifteen-year-old friend who had been born to a heroin addict, grew up on the streets, and was addicted to heroin himself. We also made our upstairs into an apartment for Diane's mother, Beth, as she got older, and eventually became her guardians as her mental and physical health failed. Later, after Beth entered a nursing home some eleven years ago, we opened our home to Frances, an aging longtime friend. Eventually, we helped her with a series of other living arrangements and managed all her affairs as her health failed.

For all the years we have cared for the special needs of others, we have done it with love. But until we became acquainted with the Twelve Steps of Alcoholics Anonymous, we also endured a great deal of emotional strain. We let ourselves become so responsible for the well-being of others, and became so wrapped up in their affairs, that we neglected ourselves. We thought that was the way it had to be. It doesn't. Little by little, as we gradually allowed the Twelve Step program into our lives, we found more and more ways to take care of ourselves. Because of this, our love and care of others now come more from a sense of fullness and joy than from a sense of duty and self-denial.

The Twelve Step program was started by a group of alcoholics in the 1930s as a way to help themselves recover from the devastation of alcoholism. They formed Alcoholics

Anonymous to share the program with one another. Since then, the principles of the program as summarized in the Twelve Steps have been adapted and applied by millions of people to other chronic problems such as compulsive overeating, gambling, and codependency. In fact, the program outlines such a practical, spiritual way of life that it has been adopted by many people who simply wish to find greater peace in their lives.

As caregivers, we found the Steps applied very well to our situation. We quickly identified with the feeling of powerlessness described in the First Step. Caregiving has often left us feeling powerless, especially over the resentment and anger it can generate. Gradually, we began to explore the program more deeply through weekly meetings with a group of other couples who found comfort and wisdom along the Twelve Step path. We have learned so much that helps us every single day as we care for others, especially those with chronic health problems.

Our longtime friend, Pat Samples, who writes about health and spiritual issues, has also adopted the Twelve Steps as an important guide in her life. In her research and writing about the needs of aging and disabled people, she saw the dilemmas faced by many caregivers and, like us, saw the Twelve Steps as an obvious resource for dealing with them. Pat came to us and asked if we would be willing to share our experience with other caregivers. We eagerly agreed.

In preparation for this book, we had many wonderful conversations with Pat about our experiences with caregiving and applying the Twelve Steps. Then Pat went on to interview numerous other caregivers who also have found the Twelve Steps a helpful guide. She used their stories, as well as ours, to help in creating this book. Its concepts are an interweaving of our ideas and hers, along with those of the other caregivers she interviewed. Pat took on the actual task of writing the book; we offered suggestions along the way. We are grateful for having shared this adventure with her because, through this sharing, the Twelve Steps have become an even richer resource for us.

Our real names are used throughout the book, and so are the names of the people we have cared for. To protect the anonymity of other caregivers who generously shared with us their very personal pain and victories, no other real names are used.

Our hope is that this book will be a source of discovery and renewed hope for you. We believe you want your caregiving to be a worthwhile and loving act that leaves you with your sanity intact. That wish may have been shattered or at least shaken a little by now. Your sense of hope for better days may have been diminished. We invite you to use this book to gain a fresh perspective on your situation, and we hope you will take the time to absorb and try out the ideas and the exercises you find here. You deserve to have the kind of life that is promised by the Twelve Steps.

Diane Larsen
Marvin Larsen

Postscript to This Introduction

The above introduction was written in 1991 when this book was first published. Both Diane's mother, Beth, and our friend, Frances, have since died, and we are no longer active caregivers on a daily basis. However, we continue to offer supportive care periodically to friends with health problems, and as the two of us face some of our own health challenges, we become caregivers for one another from time to time. We continue to value the Twelve Step program as a guide that helps us take care of ourselves when caring for others.

—September 2000

Chapter 1

What's Expected of a Caregiver

Sometimes in the spring, the rains keep coming and coming and coming for days. We try to step around the puddles, but there are no dry spots. The water rushes along everywhere, slapping up against our shoes, seeping in to wet our socks and chill our feet. Mud gets splashed on our car when we drive and on our clothes when we walk. Our hair gets damp. At times the skies seem eternally dark, although sudden eruptions of noise and light can make us shudder and run for cover. On days like these, most of us long to stay inside and wait for brighter days to come. But we don't always have that choice.

Taking care of someone with a chronic illness or disability may be a lot like these rainy times—a long-running deluge of gray days that leaves us feeling drenched in worries and responsibilities. And relief, like spring after a harsh winter and later summer, may seem a long way off. While bright moments of promise appear from time to time, choices seem limited and burdens heavy. Yet, the person receiving care needs encouragement, reassurance, and understanding. We are expected always to be there and always to be "up."

But as caregivers, we need care too. Even if we've taken

charge and are handling things quite well, the constant worry about another person's welfare, the uncertainty about what will happen next, and the day-to-day management of affairs can all be exhausting. Most of us have had our fill of answering questions, filling out forms, and endless waiting for medical diagnoses, as well as for countless decisions from doctors, hospitals, nursing homes, insurance companies, family members, and many other people. Trying to make plans while constantly monitoring symptoms and watching for relapse can test the nerves. Our jaws may become tight from trying to control both our temper and our tears while trying to get the cooperation of others.

Most likely, we hadn't expected things would turn out this way. But by now, we know that the expected can seldom be counted on when it comes to caregiving.

Parent-Child Roles May Become Partially Reversed

One day, Jean got a phone message that her mother, age eighty-three, had suffered a stroke and would probably die within a couple days. Jean prepared for the worst, but just nine days later her mother was discharged from the hospital. With her emotions in upheaval, she had to quickly find a nursing home nearby. Then, for four months Jean visited her mother twice a day, watching with agony and hope as her mother gradually recovered and eventually learned to walk and talk again. During this time, says Jean, "Our roles suddenly reversed, and I became the mother. I spooned liquids between her feverish lips, the way she did for me when I was small. I pulled the sheets up over her shoulders when she was asleep, just the way she had covered me when I was a child. She bonded with me like a baby."

Now Jean's mother is in eldercare housing back in her own hometown. Her housing arrangements include what minimal care she needs, but she makes Jean her link to the outside world. She calls Jean often to complain about her condition, to ask for pity and for help of various kinds, and to chastise Jean for not doing more for her. Jean says her mother has grown childlike. "She'll whine, 'Everybody else here has kids that come to visit them except me.' It's her way of trying to manipulate me just like I did to her when I was a teenager, when I would say, 'All the other kids get to stay out late. Why won't you let me?'" Jean feels confused and strained by this new behavior. Every day she wonders if she is doing enough for her mother, and every day she wonders if she can stand one more of those phone calls.

Putting the Focus on the Caregiver

Our situation may be similar to Jean's or different. The person each of us cares for may be older or younger, living with us or not, easy to take care of or very challenging. Whatever this person's condition or situation, *our* life has changed because of it. This book is about us and the way we respond to those changes.

Now, let's stop for a moment and take that in. The focus is on *our* needs and activities. Does this idea seem foreign? As caregivers we are used to giving attention to the person we are caring for, and we may actually find it difficult to shift that focus to ourselves for a time. That's understandable. After all, there is so much to be done. And our feelings of responsibility and concern about this other person are no doubt quite strong. We've had to operate in this reaction mode just to keep up, maybe for a long time now.

But can we allow ourselves a little time for reflection? Can we take some time to see more clearly how caring for this person is affecting us? After all, the first person we are responsible for in this life is ourselves. Maybe it's time to examine how we're handling *that* responsibility. Maybe it's time to give ourselves a break.

Let's think back to the time before we became caregivers. How was our life different then? What occupied our thoughts and our time? Let's remember the things we enjoyed, the dreams we had. What has happened to them? Chances are, our life was more our own before we became caregivers.

Then, either suddenly or over time, things may have changed. We either chose or "fell into" the role of caregiver because of the chronic physical or mental problem of someone we love. Maybe we are the primary caregiver, or maybe we are the person who gives little hands-on care, but who is depended on for decisions or other special types of help. Whatever the level of responsibility, we've usually experienced some dramatic changes, including changes in expectations.

Expectations

Caregivers are subject to a whole set of expectations. Physicians, family members, lawyers, health care administrators and workers, insurance officials, friends, employers, and the person cared for are just some of the people who look to us to respond to their concerns. The biggest expectations, however, usually come from within ourselves. We may expect ourselves to handle everything perfectly, stay in control, work long hours, keep our spirits up, know the right thing to do, put all our needs and concerns aside when someone else wants something, and more. This is a tall order for anyone to fill.

Even if we could anticipate and plan to meet all these expectations, changes and complications continually arise: The person's condition changes. The doctor changes. The insurance coverage or government regulations change. People who offer to help change their minds. The van driver for the disabled gets sick. The medication creates adverse side effects. Our job responsibilities change. Rent goes up. And there are so many decisions to make: What legal steps to take; how much time to take off work; what kind of assistance to apply for; what agencies, care facilities, or case managers are best. Someone once said, "Life is what happens when you are making other plans." How fitting for caregivers!

Some people may tell us that our responsibilities are not much different from those of most parents. It's true that raising little children does require many of the same skills and offers many of the same challenges. But there are differences. The usual expectation is that healthy children will gradually assume more responsibilities with age, and along the way, many obvious moments of growth, accomplishment, and change inspire and delight us. Parents also have many more rights concerning a child's welfare, and can exercise considerable control in many situations. Physically, small children are much easier to manage. Of course, the person we care for may also bring us many moments of delight, and health conditions can certainly improve in some cases, but more likely we are faced with accepting an ongoing and perhaps deteriorating condition.

Our days include more than difficulties, of course. Chances are we've seen progress. We've probably seen some remarkable resilience and courage on the part of the person we care for. Perhaps friends and relatives have surprised us with their willingness to help. Maybe we've found that the many resources now becoming available for the infirm and for caregivers are a godsend. No doubt we have surprised ourselves at times by how much we have been able to endure, how much we have learned, and how well we have managed—how joy in even the smallest things has transformed a cloudy day into a bright one.

In fact, many of the problems and expectations mentioned may not be that difficult for some of us. It depends on our point of view. Whether they turn out to be difficult or easy often depends a great deal on how we see them and how we respond.

As we become familiar with the Twelve Steps, we will often find different, less upsetting ways to see and respond to whatever happens as we care for another person. These ways are discussed in Chapters Three through Seven. But first, let's take a deeper look at some of the painful emotional turmoil so many caregivers experience.

Chapter 2

From the very beginning, the stresses of caregiving become obvious. We may have had to make job changes, like Sandy did. She quit her job—even though her husband, who has Alzheimer's disease, goes to a daycare facility every day. The emotional strain of dealing with him for the rest of the day was too great. Now she is in a financial pinch. Caregiving often strains the budget.

For those of us who continue working, stress piles up when there is so much to do after work—visits to make, legal matters to handle, bills to sort out, stops to make at the store to pick up that special lotion or yet another new prescription. And then there are the phone calls that come for us at work, and always we wonder *Now what?* We may have to schedule time off work to get Mother to a doctor's appointment or to rush home suddenly to handle a crisis.

An Unexpected Problem

Time becomes so precious. And despite the best of plans, things don't always go as expected. Flora remembers one day when she drove two hundred miles to her hometown to transport her mother back to her mother's house after a stay in the hospital.

By the time she reached the hospital, the long trip had made her weary. She had the usual lump in her throat. Flora would rather have made this trip just for a nice visit with her mother in the comfort of her childhood home, as she had done for so many years. But now the trips were more often for periodically transferring her mother back and forth from her stays at the hospital or nursing home. A rush of emotions tore at Flora as she approached her mother's room. She calmed herself as best she could and mentally prepared herself for the immediate task of taking her mother home. But she was not prepared for the latest twist. "I'm not going. I'm staying here!" her mother declared defiantly. Flora was flabbergasted. She had not driven two hundred miles to hear this. She was forced to exercise her own brand of defiance to keep from having her time wasted, as had happened on so many occasions before. Her mother, at last, allowed herself to be taken home.

We May Neglect Ourselves

All too often a caregiver's time seems to be wasted, causing other interests—career, family, social activities, exercise—to be neglected. We have too little time for sleep; fatigue is a daily companion.

Along with the fatigue, we often have health problems of our own. Consider Harvey, in his eighties, who cares for his wife and tries to keep up the house and yard. He is tired all the time and is losing weight. His doctor is concerned.

Likewise, Marlene has all she can do to care for Mark, her husband of fifty years, whom she has nursed through Parkinson's disease and several surgeries, cardiac arrests, and blood clots. Her parents, who are in their nineties, also call on her for help. "Mother calls me and wants me to come every day." For several months, after her parents were injured in a car accident, she did go every day. On top of all this, Marlene and Mark's daughter came "home" with her children to live for a while after leaving an abusive husband. Now Marlene had to put up with the noise and confusion of the grand-children, as well as being subjected to belligerent phone calls from her daughter's irate husband. Marlene's highly sensitive blood pressure soared.

Family relations often suffer too. Arguments can arise over who is responsible for care and how it is handled. And there is frequently little time to attend to family responsibilities, chil-dren, spouse, or others we care about.

Social Life May Be Affected

If the person receiving care is living at home with us, it can become harder to host or attend social occasions. When Nancy and her brain-injured husband would get together to visit with friends, he would pace back and forth, and he'd monopolize the conversation, repeating over and over things he forgot he had said. And if that were not enough, he was frequently the source of public embarrassment for Nancy. Once, in a store, he unzipped and took off his pants.

As caregivers, we likely have all experienced situations like these. Much attention and concern have been focused on the problems of the person we care for, but we have a great many stresses of our own. And these stresses produce plenty of emo-tional fallout. So many of us have ignored that chronic and occasional emotional pain. After all, haven't we been expected to sacrifice for the one who is disabled or infirm?

Guilt and Shame

Caregivers tend to believe everything is their fault. If only we had done something differently, the person we care for might not be in this condition. We feel *so* responsible. We think we aren't doing enough.

Marvin: When our friend Frances was living with us, she

often asked me to go out and buy her cigarettes, and I was glad to do it. I wasn't usually prepared to drop whatever I was doing at the moment she asked, just to make a special trip out, but since I often had to go out for other errands, I knew I could pick them up while I was out. But once Frances made her request, she would come back to me every hour or so and ask, in a rather demanding way, "Did you get the cigarettes yet, Marvin?" I always tried to be nice to her. I would reassure her and tell her when I planned to get them, but the next hour, there she'd be again with the same question. Pretty soon I'd start to feel guilty, and then angry. Finally, I'd just give in and go get the cigarettes.

An Old Grudge

Evelyn had once been arrested for possession of marijuana as a young woman. Her parents never forgave her for that, even years later when she had become a successful attorney and was in her forties. Her parents also frequently insisted that she donate her services to help with family legal matters, but they never expressed any appreciation and, in fact, downplayed her contributions. Her dad would lie to other family members about how poorly she had handled these matters as a way of getting back at her for her youthful indiscretion. The vicious talk about her was always behind her back; nothing was ever said directly to her.

These family patterns of holding grudges, indirectness, and ingratitude were deeply embedded. When Evelyn's mother died, her father, needing care, came to live with Evelyn and her husband. Her father's backstabbing became even more vicious. When she was away from the house, he would berate Evelyn to her husband, particularly replaying again and again the grudge over the marijuana incident from twenty years earlier. When Evelyn heard about this, she was furious, but she also was struck with guilt. "I believed I *was* the ungrateful daughter my parents always said I was." She felt obligated as a "good daughter" to take care of her father, yet resented him deeply. Each morning when she got out of bed, she would become obsessed with anger, and the feeling would grip her all day long. But she would force out a half-smiling "Good morning" to her dad, straining mightily to shield him from her true emotions.

Anger

Caregivers are often angry. So much seems unfair. So much is demanded of us. So much seems out of control. But we often feel we have no right to be angry, and then may become even more angry—at ourselves—for feeling angry. More guilt, more shame, more attempts to hide the angry feelings. But the anger shows, even when we try to keep it under control. The anger and resentment bubble up inside, creating great discomfort. Ulcers, headaches, back tension, or other physical symptoms may develop.

Chronic Grief

We normally think of feeling grief when someone dies. But it's also normal to feel sad when we experience other losses and even when we anticipate losses.

After Nancy's husband suffered brain injury at age forty-two, his personality changed completely. She lost the patient and kind husband, lover, and companion she had known. The man she took care of was a very confused, sometimes hostile and abusive stranger. She cried and mourned the loss of her husband, and so did their children, who had lost the father they knew.

Flora reacted in much the same way to her mother's deterioration. "I wanted my mother to come home from the nursing home and be my same old mother. But she wasn't very competent intellectually. I wanted to shake her back into being what I wanted her to be. But I discovered I was going to have to renegotiate the relationship because it was going to be different."

Giving What We Never Received

Old hurts can surface when, as caregivers, we find ourselves caring for a parent who had little time for us over the years. Rita only recently took on the care of her mother, whose mental acuity rapidly slipped into total confusion, making it necessary for Rita's mother to move into a nursing home. Rita is angry that she is expected to give care and affection to a mother whom she says gave little of that to her. "Sometimes I'm kind of resentful that she didn't just die. Then I think, no, I don't want her to die. I want her to be the way she was. Then maybe we could have worked out a better relationship. Now it's too late." Rita is grieving over a lifelong lack of a warm relationship with her mother. Now, as she says, it's too late.

The Way It Was

Even changes in the physical environment can generate a startling sense of loss at times. One Thanksgiving, Flora had gone home to her mother's house. It felt good to be "home" again. Sure, it was Flora's job now, instead of her mother's, to prepare the turkey and the dressing and the cranberries, but at least her mother was not in the nursing home for this favorite holiday; she was home where she belonged. For the moment, Flora set aside the twinge she felt every time she peered inside "her" room—the bedroom of her childhood that her mother had kept just the way Flora liked it from the time Flora had left home. Now the room belonged to the home health aide; Flora's stuffed animals and high school photos had been packed away.

Beginning meal preparations in the kitchen, Flora felt more at home. She opened the cupboard to reach for the pans she needed. They were not in their usual place. She couldn't find the baster. The foods in the refrigerator were not the familiar ones her mother had always kept there. Flora stopped for a moment, her heart fluttering. It dawned on her that the aide and her mother's friends who had been helping her mother had altered the familiar kitchen arrangements. In that moment, Flora was suddenly pierced with sadness. "I realized my mother was no longer in charge of her own home," Flora recalls. "She wasn't doing those things that made her my mom. Other people were making the decisions." Her mother's loss was also a loss for Flora—a subtle one, but painfully real.

It is normal to feel sad when we lose someone or something precious. In our role as caregivers, we may lose not only our old relationship with the person we care for, but other comfortable connections as well. Some of our freedom, our time, our sleep, our friends, and our peace of mind may also slip away.

Depression

For some caregivers, the losses are too great, the pressures too many. They sink into depression. But other things may contribute to the depression. Someone who stays at home all the time to care for an infirm spouse or parent or child may become isolated, bored, tired. Karen's and Evelyn's situations are good examples.

For years Karen has had a bitter relationship with her mother, who now lives in a nursing home. Karen struggled with a self-hatred that she learned from a harsh upbringing. This set the stage for a depression so severe that Karen was unwilling, at times, to leave home or meet new people.

Evelyn wanted so much to receive appreciation from her

father, and got only criticism. The strain became too great for her. On the verge of depression, she finally sought counseling.

Jealousy

The jealousy we caregivers tend to feel is often a surprise to us. But when we see the person we care for always being the center of attention, jealousy is a natural reaction.

Nancy was overwhelmed with this emotion one Sunday morning. As she filed out of church, Nancy saw the outstretched hand of the pastor reaching toward her. In the previous tense weeks, again and again she had had to intervene in the illogical actions of her brain-injured spouse as he fertilized the lawn over and over and demanded that she show him how to use a computer program he couldn't possibly comprehend. Nancy was eager for a word of comfort and reassurance from the pastor that would help her go on. But, as usual, he asked only about her husband, apparently oblivious to her anguish. She never went back to that church.

Embarrassment

Embarrassment is such an uncomfortable feeling, and it almost always takes us by surprise. The person we care for may stumble, spill something or knock something over, have unpleasant odors, or use uncharacteristic vulgar language. He or she may become belligerent, fail to recognize friends or relatives, become loud and demanding, or lack bowel or bladder control. Even though we know the person isn't responsible and we can do little, if anything, to control him or her, we still feel embarrassed. People stare, question, pull away, make rude or naive remarks. It's awkward, to say the least. We often feel deeply responsible for the person's behavior, and the shame may become so overwhelming that we do everything we can to keep him or her hidden away from the public, increasing our isolation and loneliness as well.

Related to embarrassment, but even more uncomfortable, are feelings of repulsion.

Nancy had to deal with such feelings as she found the vulgar, demanding, impatient man who emerged from the coma after the accident to be "disgusting." His attempts at initiating sex were "about as awkward as a twelve-year-old boy's."

Flora, too, had to fight feelings of repulsion. In addition to caring for her infirm mother, Flora provided care for a man in her apartment building who was dying of AIDS. He had been abandoned by his family and friends; the physical effects of the disease were almost more than she could bear to be around. The man had endured severe sexual abuse since boyhood, and he poured out his life story of agony and hurt to Flora, a good listener. "I couldn't take much of it at any one time," she says. "I felt like I was going crazy, like I wanted to scream, 'Stop!' But I knew I was the only person this guy had ever had to talk to about these things. I would just excuse myself when it became too much for me."

Denial

Flora marvels at how hard it has been for her to face the fact that her mother is losing her ability to think clearly. "Denial is such a mystery," she says. She knows denial is commonplace, but she is always surprised to find it in herself. Since Flora is a hospital chaplain working with dying people and with chemically dependent people, she knows that denial is a normal reaction when a person doesn't want to face a disease. Flora knows a lot *about* denial. Yet, that hasn't kept her from experiencing it herself. "I try to be thoughtful, and I'm a reasonably intelligent person. But it's hard to look at your own parents becoming incompetent."

In the journal she keeps, she has noticed the patterns of denial that show up over and over again. "For a long time, I tried to deny our relationship had changed," she says. What she noticed in her writings, she says, is that "I would get so furious with my mother over and over because she seemed to have everything anyone at her age could want—a nice home, a son living nearby, lots of concerned friends—and yet she couldn't seem to do the simple things she needed to do to keep her independence. She would refuse sometimes to even get out of bed. I kept insisting that she stop being so anxious and depressed and get herself well. I was unwilling to accept the fact that she couldn't."

In addition to denying the condition of our loved ones, it is also easy to deny our own feelings about what is happening. As caregivers, many of us like to see ourselves as strong, competent, able to manage things. Emotions are considered nuisances that get in our way and are best ignored. Still, we feel them. They come out either directly or indirectly. We may get angry at someone at work, when what we are really angry about is all the added responsibility at home or the lack of appreciation we get for the care we are giving. We may find ourselves crying uncontrollably over a movie, when the real sadness comes from our feelings of personal loss.

These are some of the feelings that caregivers experience. Some caregivers may be familiar with other feelings not mentioned here. Of course, we also experience positive feelings— relief when there are improvements, satisfaction from being able to be of service, and admiration for the courage we witness, among others. Sometimes we are even afraid to feel these positive emotions because we fear they won't last, or because our anger or jealousy or denial stands in the way.

Caregiving can seem like a jumble with all these difficulties and all these feelings cropping up. The chronic emotional pain we feel can overwhelm us, or at least threaten to. Sometimes we run and hide from it, and sometimes there is no place to hide.

Chapter 3

The Twelve Step program of Alcoholics Anonymous offers a way to respond to life's crises, whether they are caused by addictions or by other deeply troubling conditions or circumstances such as caregiving. The program has been used by millions of people to chart a spiritual path for daily living with very practical implications.

Those of us caregivers who draw upon this program find strength and hope in the midst of daily trials. It helps us to live one day at a time. The program equips us to change what we can and find peace with what we can't. Little by little, we are able to see beyond our obvious problems to some of the deeper causes for the tremendous emotional turmoil we experience. We cut loose the restraints that hold us back from a full and rich life. We learn to embrace the present moment, whether faced with agonizing decisions, uncontrollable circumstances, or day-to-day tedium. We can access a deep joy.

The Twelve Step program is not a fast fix-it recipe that we master after going over it once or twice. In fact, speed doesn't count at all. Rather, it's an ongoing program for living. We proceed through the Twelve Steps many times, taking all the time we need, each time deepening our spirituality and our joy.

We call on the wisdom of each Step as needed in our day-to-day living.

In the following chapters, we explore each of the Twelve Steps, one at a time. The Steps discussed are an adaptation of the Twelve Steps of Alcoholics Anonymous. We call them the Twelve Steps for caregivers, and they are printed in their entirety in Appendix Two on page 139. Following a discussion of each Step are one or more exercises to help deepen our understanding and apply the Step to our life.

Take some time with them. Slow down to fully absorb their impact.

You may want to keep a journal for the written exercises, and for writing other thoughts, feelings, and observations as you progress through the Steps. You will find a journal a valuable companion. Among other benefits, it can help you stay focused on the process, sort out troublesome issues, see patterns that may be helping or hindering you, and remember important discoveries.

STEP ONE: We admitted we were powerless over the people we are taking care of—that our lives had become unmanageable.

The First Step asks us to admit the powerlessness we experience in caregiving. At first, this notion may seem appalling, even frightening. We want to be in control of the situations in our life. We may even pride ourselves on being able to manage things quite well. We do our best to keep on top of things, meet everyone's expectations, keep up with all the changes, untangle messy complications, control our temper, and keep our sanity.

A moment may come, however, when everything seems out of control, when no one is cooperating, when plans are not working out, when we feel completely lost. Moments like these, as painful as they may be, are also a gift. They can bring into clear focus the fact that we are powerless over many of the circumstances in our life as caregivers, that we can't change someone else's illness, that we can't change how anyone thinks or behaves—nor much of anything outside of ourselves.

Even when we try to change ourselves—our thoughts, our habits, our desires—we may find ourselves stymied. How many times have we experienced a great sense of powerlessness when trying to control our diet, our procrastination, perhaps our smoking, our temper, or our tongue? And how often have our attempts to control a situation ended up alienating people and leaving us completely exhausted because they just wouldn't cooperate? Although we may feel more secure when we can take charge of a situation, so often there is simply nothing we can do about it. And what we try to do just creates a new set of problems.

Diane: When my mother, Beth, was diagnosed with Alzheimer's, I had a great deal of difficulty accepting the diagnosis. I felt very helpless. I frantically sought a series of other medical opinions. I worked with my mother on her memory every day, sitting her down again and again, trying to get her to write her name. I was determined to fight the diagnosis. It just couldn't be. I gritted my teeth and decided she would *get better.*

Marvin: For a long time, I also resisted the inevitable deterioration of the disease. I felt that, with enough effort, we at least should be able to slow its progress. When we decided Beth would come and live with us, everyone in our household agreed to work with her to keep her oriented. When I was gone to work and the children were in school, Diane would work diligently with Beth, drilling her on what time of day it was and what was happening that day, trying desperately to stop the progress of the disease.

Diane: *I became frustrated and angry and resentful because my mother was not responding. Her condition was getting worse. I remember once, when I had several couples over for a Christmas brunch, my mother came up with the notion that I was going to move away and leave her. She began to sob, pleading with me, "Please don't move. What will I do? Where will I go?" It was all I could do not to cry myself. I ended up spending an hour in the kitchen, away from my guests, trying to convince her I wasn't going to move away.*

Before long, I had put Beth first in my life. I stole time from my family. I put Marvin and the children on the back burner. I'd get back spasms because I was so tense about Mother's health. I'd be laid up in bed for several days.

Marvin: *We all rallied around to help Diane. I took over a lot of the household chores. But everyone, Diane included, was resentful a lot of the time. We felt powerless.*

Many caregivers have similar situations. For example, maybe some of us made a promise never to put our relative or friend in a nursing home. Then the promise seemed impossible to keep. Some of us may feel that we owe certain things to this person or that we must prove ourselves a devoted and worthy child or friend. Maybe we are just plain tired at the end of the day and can't stand the thought of giving that last bit of care for the day—putting someone to bed or making that good-night phone call. Maybe we're just plain mad that we're stuck with all this, and yet feel guilty about feeling that way.

Powerlessness

Circumstances such as these leave the most capable, confident person feeling powerless. The emotional pain rolls in like waves; we try our best, but we can't stop it.

The First Step for caregivers, then, is to acknowledge our powerlessness—over the people we are caring for, over the illness, over the surrounding circumstances, over all the emotional anguish that results. It is a way to fully grasp just how unmanageable our life has become.

By itself, this notion of powerlessness could produce only despair. But it is only the First Step. And in the end, it is a great relief. It means we no longer *have* to be in charge. We can let go of the obsessive drive, so common in caregivers, to manage and control everything. We can stop being the one who is responsible for everything turning out right. A heavy burden is lifted.

> *The Larsens: Nothing our family did—despite our frenzied determination—changed the outcome for Grandma Beth. Eventually her brain deteriorated so badly that she was unable to communicate or to move on her own. She lived in a nursing home for over a decade.*

> *Diane: But gradually, through working the First Step, I learned to let go. I gave myself permission not to go to the nursing home as often. I realized I could not "save" her, and I could not make her the center of my life. Earlier, even when she could no longer recognize me or communicate, I felt obligated to go often. With every visit, I became more depressed and resentful. Why does this have to happen to her? I want her back. On Mother's Day, for several years, I stayed home. But gradually, through working the First Step, I have been learning to let go. I am giving myself permission to not go to the nursing home so often. I*

realize I cannot save her, and I cannot make her the center of my life.

One year I was able to go see my mother on Mother's Day. I had joined an Alzheimer's support group, and through their encouragement and tremendous empathy, I began to see my mother in a different light. I strode into the nursing home knowing that I would hold her and talk to her, even though she could not respond.

When I walked into her room, I noticed how tiny she looked, curled in the fetal position that is so typical of Alzheimer's patients in the final stage. I had bought a pink orchid because pink had always looked so becoming on her. I walked over to the side of the bed, and pinned the orchid on her gown. It was much too big for her frail body. I massaged her brow, spoke to her softly, and as I did so, my tears poured out, landing on the orchid. I felt myself letting go. I knew it was okay to cry.

In looking back, if we had understood the First Step earlier, we might have been able to give up being the primary caregivers for Beth sooner. As it was, Beth had lost all bowel and bladder control. At the dinner table, she would get confused and start to cry. Our family mealtimes tended to get shorter. Our teenage children found excuses to be away from home a great deal. If we had been honest, perhaps we could have seen that Beth might have been better off in a quieter place, rather than in the whirlwind of our very active family life. We probably hung on too long, thinking that somehow, if we tried hard enough, we could compensate for Beth's misfortune.

To caregivers, the First Step is about freedom, the freedom to accept what is really happening and experience it fully—emotional pain and all. This Step gives us a way to stop denying it, hiding from it, or trying to move away from it. We no longer have to control it, to hold it all in check. We can be free of this heavy responsibility. As we release ourselves from these efforts to be in control, we can also begin to free ourselves from letting all the circumstances of caregiving control us as well. We are on our way to finding a Power greater than life's circumstances, greater than ourselves.

EXERCISE: THE UNMANAGEABLE LOAD

On a sheet of paper, begin drawing a pile of big rocks—any kind of circles will do just fine. Draw one rock for each thing or person you are now trying to control in your life—perhaps someone's behavior or your finances or schedule. Take your time and be as specific as possible, including a rock for everything small and large that you are trying to manage. Label the rocks. When you are finished, observe how large the pile is. Imagine these rocks loaded into a bag, and then imagine trying to lift it and carry it around with you all the time. Go ahead and experience for a moment just how heavy this feels. Imagine carrying it for as long as you have been a caregiver. Think for a moment about whether you are really in charge of this load, or whether it is, in fact, controlling your life. When the load becomes unmanageable, set it down. Leave it there.

The First Step is like that, letting go of your load. If you are used to being very responsible, this exercise may be quite difficult. Yet, only by laying down your load will you find it possible to experience a much greater source of Power who will carry the load for you. Let Go and Let God.

STEP TWO: Came to believe that a Power greater than ourselves could restore us to sanity.

Step Two starts us on a profound spiritual path that leads to trusting in a Power beyond ourselves—a Power we can turn to for peace of mind. Some of us may be put off by this notion. Maybe we don't believe in God, or maybe our faith has been shattered or set aside. Whatever our point of view, no doubt we have a good reason for it. Whether we are already comfortable with trusting in God or are alienated in some way, we can consider taking a fresh look at the idea of *spirituality*.

As expressed in Step Two, the Power greater than ourselves may be God (however we define God), or it may be another source of power such as nature, a support group, or our common sense—whatever we believe will look out for our best interests and help us with our problems. This is not a harsh, condemning power. Rather, this Higher Power, as it is often called, is filled with wisdom and love. If we have trouble finding a Higher Power we can believe in, we can trust in the Twelve Step program itself. It has become a source of great healing and serenity for millions of people, and for that reason alone, it may be enough of a Higher Power in the beginning.

Defining Our Higher Power

For many people, their Higher Power is God. If we come from a strong religious tradition and have a longtime commitment to our faith, taking this Step may not appear that difficult.

> *The Larsens: When we first became acquainted with the Twelve Steps, we already believed that God uses power, wisdom, and love to care for us and guide us. Over time, however, we have come to appreciate even more deeply what this means to us as caregivers. We see the word "believe" as an action word. With this belief, we can let go of our worries—completely. We can trust that all our concerns will be taken care of lovingly by God, even when we can't understand the outcome, or don't like it. Our belief in this wise and loving Power assures us that peace of mind is there waiting for us at all times. Again and*

again, the two of us have found this to be true.

Both of us believe that, just as we are cared for by a Higher Power, so are all others. That means we don't have the ultimate responsibility for anyone's feelings, thoughts, or behavior. Knowing this can be a big relief. When our friend Frances left our home and lived in a senior citizen high-rise for a while, we did everything we could to remind her not to carelessly leave lit cigarettes lying around as she had often done in our home, and we notified the building manager of the potential danger. At first, we worried about this a lot, but eventually we realized we had done all we could, and the rest was in God's hands.

Taking Step Two may be harder if we reject or are ill at ease with the ideas of God and spirituality. We may even be very angry at God. We may blame God for bringing on another's health problems and for burdening us with added responsibilities and emotional pain. Some people feel God is punishing them for something they have done. When we have these thoughts and feelings, we are not alone.

Karen Learned to Trust Again

Karen's father was a minister who preached love, but beat her as a child and inflicted other cruelties on her. Her mother, too, treated her harshly. Karen had trouble making sense out of the conflicting messages she got from all this. She still carries a lot of fear with her. All her life, it has been hard for her to trust anyone, let alone God. In the Twelve Step program, she found the support she needed to begin trusting again. She got familiar with the program when her husband went through treatment for alcoholism. Now she uses the Steps to help her keep her sanity in dealing with her invalid mother, who still criticizes her heavily.

Odella Found Her Spirituality Deep Within

Waiting in the clinic each time her small daughter underwent chemotherapy, Odella would observe and talk with other families. She noticed anxious parents who thought if they prayed hard enough and were good enough, God would reward them with the health of their child. "I never did," Odella says. "In the beginning, I thought in the traditional style of God as a father, but I've changed my mind about that. Now I just think of God as a merciful, warm, kind presence who walks with us, suffers *with* us. I started accepting that 'what will be, will be,' and that I will have the strength to endure whatever has to be endured."

Odella also shifted away from the religion-based, church-going spirituality she had grown up with. "I had to reach deeper within myself and define it in a more personal, spiritual way. It went from being an external thing to being a real internal thing."

At times, Odella got mad at God. "I went through periods when I couldn't even pray. I thought it wasn't fair. I had to work hard to fight self-pity. I found out that self-pity did nothing but hurt me, so I couldn't indulge in that."

Evelyn Was Helped by Al-Anon

Evelyn had adopted the "God is dead" philosophy popular in the 1960s. "I considered myself an atheist. I thought everybody was responsible for themselves, that things just happened, without a plan. I had a real hard time with 'Higher Power.'" This view kept Evelyn from feeling very comfortable with Al-Anon, the support group for families of alcoholics that she had attended a few times when her husband went through treatment. But later, when her father moved in with her, Evelyn went back to Al-Anon out of desperation. And she groped for a way to understand the idea of a Power greater than herself.

"Now my Higher Power is just a sense that I'm not in control of the whole world. It's sort of a sense of balance at work. I'm not real sure what it is, but I'm content to not figure it out. I can just trust that things are going to turn out all right. It took the burden off me of being responsible for everything that happened to me."

That's the heart of the matter—feeling responsible for everything. Our self-will, our ego, is at work when we believe this. We want to be in charge. We think we know what's best. As caregivers, we often think no one can do things as well as we can. But if we are honest with ourselves, we will admit that even when we are in charge, things get out of hand. They get downright crazy at times.

Defining Insanity

No matter what she did, Nancy's brain-injured husband would forget that he had just eaten a meal and would sit down again to eat. He would plant grass seed on the lawn's bare spots and then go out and sprinkle water on them over and over, all day long. During the time he was in a wheelchair, he sometimes tried to go down the stairs.

Nancy felt she was completely responsible for controlling all this behavior. She took what precautions she could, of course, such as putting a gate in front of the stairs, but so many things happened that she could not control. She wanted everything to get back to normal, and it couldn't. Gradually, the children began acting out at school, and Nancy's personality changed to the point where friends and relatives began to notice. She didn't sleep well. Her husband's safety was a constant worry. An occasional cigarette became two packs a day. She withdrew into herself.

This is the kind of craziness or "insanity" that Step Two talks about. We become so obsessed with the other person's needs and behavior that we lose ourselves. With only our own ego steering us, with our self-will trying so hard to run things, we spin ourselves into a hole. We give in to resentment, self-pity, fear, blame, and depression. Like Karen, who feels like "clunking my mother in the head," we get to the same place of frustration; or like another caregiver, Laura, we fall in love with the married guy next door in order to feel better.

Step Two gives us a way to restore our sanity. We are asked to take a chance on believing that a Higher Power could relieve us of all this anxiety, this craziness. This belief can lead to a state of serenity. We can stop fretting about the future and assigning blame for the past. Though Karen still feels some anger toward her mother, she now turns to her Higher Power to calm herself when she is upset. She is more relaxed when she visits her mother and enjoys listening to her stories. Laura, whose marriage became rocky after her ailing mother moved in, no longer looks to romance outside her marriage to soothe her troubled spirit. Both Karen and Laura are healing from the hurts of the past through counseling and the support of their husbands and friends.

Living a sane life means living One Day at a Time. For caregivers, sometimes it's a matter of just hanging on from moment to moment. We wait for the doctor's word after another test or procedure. We get another phone call from that one relative who always upsets us. We try to go to sleep, wondering if our father or spouse will get up and wander around and get hurt. The stresses are many, but we can find serenity each moment, day by day, if we are willing to take Step Two.

EXERCISE: A MIND GAME

Take a few moments to relax and play a little mind game. It will help you exercise your power of concentration, as a way to better understand Step Two. For the greatest benefit, do this exercise as you read it, one sentence at a time, rather than first reading it all the way through.

Look around the room until you find a chair or piece of furniture that has legs on it. Study the legs; notice their shape, their color, their size. If you can, move your hands over them. Are they cold or warm? What is their texture? Tap or wiggle them a little and listen to the sound. Imagine how these legs were made and where the materials came from.

If you followed these directions, for at least a few minutes your attention was taken away from the person you care for and from worries associated with your caregiving. You concentrated only on the furniture legs. We hope the experience was pleasurable.

In the same way, anytime you feel a little bit crazy, whenever things seem out of control, you can take your attention away from whatever is causing that feeling and concentrate on your Higher Power. This Power is greater than any of those circumstances and greater than your feelings. You can call on this resource to replace your ego's self-destructive thoughts and feelings with positive, reassuring ones.

EXERCISE: DEFINING YOUR HIGHER POWER

One way to develop the habit of turning to your Higher Power is to practice doing it. Frequently pay attention to your Higher Power, whether this is God or some other source, until the practice becomes second nature to you. Here is a way to begin.

Take a few quiet moments and write out your definition of a Higher Power in as much detail as you can. Try to identify some positive, concrete image or feeling you associate with that Power. It may be some religious symbol, such as a statue. It may be a feeling of warmth near your heart. It may be a bright white light surrounding you.

Whatever comes to mind, try drawing a picture of it. Notice the feelings associated with the drawing. Listen. Apply all of your senses, as well as your imagination, to fully appreciate the presence of your Higher Power at this moment. You will want to become very familiar with this Power—your source of strength, hope, and peace of mind. The more comfortable and trusting you become, the better you will be prepared to take Step Three.

> STEP THREE: Made a decision to turn our will and our lives over to the care of God as we understood God.

Step Three asks us to surrender our will and our life to our Higher Power. That's a tall order for caregivers, especially if we are strong-minded. To go from being in charge and being super-responsible to a position of surrender can seem like a monumental shift. It is monumental in some ways, but it does not have to be hard. It is a natural outgrowth of Steps One and Two. First, we recognize we are powerless, and then we put our faith in a Higher Power that can restore our sanity. The next step is to release the controls and turn them over to God. Let Go and Let God is the simple concept that guides us.

The Meaning of Surrender

Some of us are afraid of the notion of surrender. It implies that we are losing a battle or becoming too passive. In Step Three, surrender means neither loss nor passivity, but rather an active acceptance of what *is*. People who go white-water rafting soon learn that riding *with* the waves makes for the smoothest trip. A sailing ship only makes progress when the sails are turned to pick up the wind. Step Three is not a matter of surrendering to people or circumstances and letting them control us. Rather, we surrender to our Higher Power, who will lovingly guide our ship if we release the controls.

Harvey learned to apply the principle of surrender. His

wife, who has Alzheimer's, sometimes likes to take a package of cheese to bed with her at night. Harvey does not waste energy being upset or arguing with her. He just waits until she is asleep and then returns the cheese to the refrigerator.

She Learned Acceptance

Because surrender implicitly means giving up control, Odella half jokes that "I had to learn to lead my life *out of control.*" When her daughter, Marietta, was first diagnosed with leukemia at age five, Odella had an overwhelming need to be in control. She kept a detailed notebook tracking every test and its results. She begged friends to keep their children from saying anything to Marietta about her condition. "I would focus on things that weren't really important, thinking I was in control. But I wasn't." After a year of this, says Odella, "I figured out I couldn't really be in control." She began to surrender, accepting whatever came and trusting that God was walking with her.

It was only through this acceptance and trust in God that Odella was able to keep her peace of mind during Marietta's treatment while making the frequent trips to a clinic over sixty miles away, a drive on a treacherous road nicknamed "Killer Highway." Of greater concern was leaving behind her other two small children with whatever friends or baby-sitters were available. "Hospitalizations were for two weeks a lot of times, which meant that each morning I'd go stay with her, so I would have to have a different friend stay with my other kids each day. I remember this older lady who tried so hard to make my two-and-a-half-year-old son like her. She even sat in the sandbox and played with him. But he would not respond to her. He could only respond to the fact that Momma was going again. He would just stand there crying, called her 'Ishy Miller' (her name was Mrs. Miller), and she would just be heartbroken, and so would I. I would drive out of our subdivision and, for I don't know how many miles, I'd be crying, thinking of my little two-and-a-half-year-old that I had left." Despite such anguish, Odella decided early on that lingering self-pity would only make her feel worse, and she refused to hang on to it.

At the clinic, she wanted so much to hear reassurances from the doctors about Marietta, but there were none. They were trying something new and could make no predictions. Even when they did make predictions (the first prognosis for life expectancy was six months), Odella still had no control. Not over the results of the treatment, including all the nausea, pain, and hair loss. Not over the weeks in the hospital. Not over the cancelled family vacations or other often-changed plans. Not over how long Marietta would live. She surrendered it all, accepting whatever came, including the anger, impatience, sadness, and other painful emotions. It was fifteen years after the diagnosis (and several years after the doctors thought Marietta had been cured) that Odella's daughter died.

During all that time, Odella felt God walking with her, giving her strength. Though she experienced much difficulty and sadness, she wasted little time worrying or wishing she had done something differently.

"I found out that the best I could do was get through One Day at a Time." She developed an interest in needlework, an activity she could work on both at home and at the clinic. She also began taking all three children on the trips to the clinic, and included fun stops at museums and parks along the way. The family went on camping trips when Marietta was in remission. Odella turned to good friends for support when things seemed overwhelming. She enjoyed each day that Marietta lived. She encouraged the lively and outgoing child to do the same, allowing Marietta to do all the normal childhood activities she felt well enough to do.

One day, Marietta begged her mother to get the child's bike out in the early spring. Odella hesitated because there were still some icy patches on the streets and Marietta's medication made her bones fragile. Mother and daughter talked it over and together they decided to take the risk.

No more than ten minutes passed before the phone rang. It was a neighbor: "Guess what?" Odella braced herself. "Marietta took a fall. She hurt her ankle and I think it's broken." The anxiety Odella felt passed as soon as she got to her daughter's side. "Marietta and I had talked it over and we had agreed we were willing to take that risk, so we just both kind of laughed and said, 'That one didn't work, did it?'" Marietta had learned the Third Step spirit of acceptance from her mother, a spirit Odella describes as "open honesty and not avoiding the pain."

Denial

How often we try to avoid pain by denying it is there! If someone asks with sincere interest how we are doing, we tend to answer "fine" and change the subject. When tears start to come, we may try to hide them, feeling we have to tough it out, fearful someone will think less of us. If we get angry, we may feel embarrassed.

"I think it's hard to be in *full* denial when you have a child who is dying," says Odella, "because so many things pull you out of it, so many things have to be done. But it is awfully easy not to acknowledge the grief, and the fact that this is so painful that you almost don't know where to turn. It would be very easy to put on a stone face and try to be strong and think *I will not talk about this; I will just steel myself and get through this*. But, if you do that, down the road, you cheat yourself so terribly, and you never start really healing. I think to get to real healing and to end up as a whole person, you have to have that honesty and you have to go through those stages."

We don't have to be alarmed or embarrassed when we find ourselves experiencing denial. Denial is a natural way of protecting ourselves whenever we face losses, addictions, or other emotionally troubling situations.

What can be dangerous is staying in denial indefinitely, obstinately refusing to acknowledge what is happening or what could happen. Some of us insist we can take personal care of a loved one, even when it's obvious that his or her condition has deteriorated so much that only trained professionals can provide appropriate care. Others, fearful of outside opinions, may refuse any kind of help from friends or family, even when we feel greatly burdened.

There is a certain ego in being a "caring person." We often find it hard to let go of that. If we don't live up to that image, what will people think? With God in charge, the ego can take a lifelong vacation. Once we surrender, what becomes important is not what other people think or what we ourselves want, but God's will.

Accepting Life As Is

One of the storytellers in the book *Alcoholics Anonymous,* commonly known as the "Big Book," says, "Unless I accept life completely on life's terms, I cannot be happy. I need to concentrate not so much on what needs to be changed in the world as on what needs to be changed in me and in my attitudes."*

Sometimes accepting life means accepting all the fears we have that keep us from taking action. We caregivers may practice denial by saying we don't have time to go see Mother or we're sure she'll snap out of this pretty soon, when what we mean is that we are afraid to face the truth about her situation. Her decline may remind us of our own mortality. We may also be afraid of facing all the difficulties that have strained our relationship. If we have been at odds with our parents for years, we may say we don't care what

Alcoholics Anonymous, 3d ed. (New York: AA World Services, Inc., 1976), 449. Reprinted with permission of AA World Services, Inc.

happens to them, denying the deep hurt we feel.

Another way we try to mask our feelings is to blame somebody else for what happens: *If only my brother or sister weren't so selfish. . . . If only dad weren't so stubborn. . . . If only the doctors had done something differently.*

We also blame ourselves: *If only we had tried harder. . . . If only we weren't so stupid. . . . If only we had gotten there sooner.*

Does any of this masking—denial or blaming—give us peace of mind?

Those of us who work the Twelve Steps have found that when we deny our feelings or try to blame someone for our problems, we become more and more disturbed. To again quote the Big Book, "When I am disturbed, it is because I find some person, place, thing, or situation—some fact of my life—unacceptable to me, and I can find no serenity until I accept that person, place, thing, or situation as being exactly the way it is supposed to be at this moment. Nothing, absolutely nothing happens in God's world by mistake."*

In the act of surrender, we align ourselves with God's will, with the way things are. We stop thinking we know better than God, and accept everything that comes to us as a gift from God.

This act of surrender is something we can do every day. At especially challenging times, we may make the decision to surrender many, many times during the day.

The Twelve Step program offers us the Serenity Prayer as a simple, but powerful tool to help us do that. Some of us use it to put to rest our fears and anxiety. It frees us to be completely honest and to be at peace with whatever comes our way.

> *God, grant me the serenity*
> *To accept the things I cannot change,*
> *The courage to change the things I can,*
> *And the wisdom to know the difference.*

Alcoholics Anonymous, 3d ed. (New York: AA World Services, Inc., 1976), 449. Reprinted with permission of AA World Services, Inc.

EXERCISE: MAKING LEMONADE

Have you ever heard this riddle?

Q: What do you do if life hands you a lemon?
A: Make lemonade.

That's a lighthearted example of what it means to surrender. The idea is this: Take what you get and make the best of it. You've probably done this many times in your life already. And sometimes, even without your effort, things that appeared worrisome turned out for the best. These exercises can help you get better acquainted with the notion of surrender and help you release your worries.

Get out some paper and a pen, your imagination, and your memory. Make three columns on a sheet of paper.

In the first column, list everything you can remember that you worried about in the last month or, if you prefer, in the last year. Make a complete list.

In the second column, put a check mark by those items that turned out all right in the end.

In the third column, put a check mark by those items that benefited from your worrying about them. Put a plus sign after those items that worked out once you let go of the controls and accepted them. Take some time to remember the moment of surrender and how it felt. Congratulate yourself. Know that the more you practice surrendering, the more natural it will become.

Chances are, the third column will have no check marks, because worrying doesn't help us solve anything. Notice the number of things in the second column that turned out well whether or not you worried. As to the events that didn't turn out the way you wanted them to, look at them again and see if there were *any* positive outcomes. Could there still be some? What could you do to create some?

Ask your Higher Power for help with this.

Make three columns on another sheet of paper. In the first column, list all the things you are now worried about, especially those that pertain to caregiving. Now ask yourself: *Can any of these really be helped by worrying?* Ask for guidance from your Higher Power concerning your worries. Then use the following process to make decisions about each one.

For now, skip the second column, but *in the third column, write out a specific plan of action for the things you can change.* This does not mean taking control, however. Instead, plan to do what you can, but then surrender the outcome to your Higher Power.

For each item on your list that you don't think you can change, take some time to imagine the best possible outcome. Write it down in the second column.

Now return to the third column and *ask your Higher Power for help in bringing about the outcome you picture.* Write down any ideas that come to you now. Make specific plans for those you wish to act on. Again, surrender the outcomes to your Higher Power. Remember, your Higher Power may have better plans in mind.

If you still have some things on your list that can't be changed, ask your Higher Power to help you accept them. See if you can make "lemonade" out of any of them.

Chapter 4

Acknowledging What Hurts

STEP FOUR: Made a searching and fearless moral inventory of ourselves.

Think for a moment about how you put on your shoes when you get dressed: Do you first put on the left shoe or your right one? Chances are, you do it the same way every day. It's become a matter of habit. Yet you may not have noticed this habit until just now. We are unaware of many of our habits. Some things, we have been doing for many years, and we just take it for granted that that's the way to do those things.

Some of our habits serve us well. For example, being responsible and getting adequate rest help us carry out our role as caregivers. Other habits may keep creating problems. Constantly demanding perfection of ourselves and others keeps us disappointed and frustrated.

Most of us can only partially identify our good and bad habits. Some of us may be reluctant to acknowledge the positive things we do and concentrate instead on fretting over what we do "wrong." Others of us may brag about our good qualities, but become annoyed, even irate, at the suggestion that we have shortcomings. Whatever perspective we have on our behaviors, we usually see an incomplete picture. We may never have stopped to consider them or we may be afraid of seeing a complete picture. It may mean there is something about us that needs changing. And changing habits can seem like hard work. But if we are honest, we likely will admit that keeping some of our habits (self-pity or blaming, for example) is also hard work, because they create so much ongoing pain and frustration.

Step Four asks us to stop and think about our habits and how they affect others as well as ourselves. This is called doing a moral inventory. It is an important step for caregivers because it allows us to look at the difficulties associated with caregiving in a fresh light. It's a little like spring house-cleaning. We dust off and polish the things we like as they are, and we repair, redecorate, or throw away the rest. By thoroughly reviewing our difficulties and how we have responded to them, we can begin to see and appreciate our positive habits of caring and competency. We also shed light on our self-destructive behaviors and the harmful ways we treat others—ways that may have left us feeling ineffective and unhappy. We can acknowledge the fears, the loneliness, the anger, the jealousy, the chronic grief, the dishonesty, the embarrassment—all the feelings and actions that cause us pain and get us into trouble.

Resistance to Doing an Inventory

Many of us feel some resistance to doing an inventory. We may think we're pretty nice and wonder why we should be concerned with what few things we do that might bother others. At the same time, listing our good qualities may seem arrogant. Overall, we may believe that a moral inventory could be good for someone who really needs it, but not for us. We may feel that whatever problems we have are caused by others or by the conditions in our life, not by anything we are doing.

Or some of us get quickly mired in guilt and self-loathing when we think about our shortcomings. We may despair at ever changing. We may even get depressed and withdraw from others, filled with shame.

Whatever the reasons, feeling resistant to doing an inventory is neither right nor wrong. But by acknowledging our resistance, we can learn something from it. It might be a form of denial. Throughout our life we tend to develop habits of denial to protect ourselves, to cope with uncomfortable things happening within and around us. Seeing an inventory as something meant only for other people might be a disguise for a self-righteousness that we developed to feel good about ourselves at a time when underneath we felt unloved or insecure. Feeling depression and despair about being unable to change might be another habit of denial we developed because the people around us didn't believe in us or stood in our way.

If we take an honest look at how we approach doing an inventory, we can eventually let our reluctance go and begin doing the inventory itself. Honesty is important to doing a searching and fearless moral inventory. When we're honest, Step Four can be such a gift. If we are willing, we will uncover some important new truths about ourselves, and with truth comes freedom. We will be free to make choices based on what is, not on our partially shielded or well-hidden version of reality.

Marvin: For a long time I resented our friend Frances because she would manipulate me into doing things I really didn't want to do. I thought I shouldn't feel like that, but I did feel that way. And in my upbringing, I had been taught that you didn't talk back to older people. I thought if I reacted to Frances, I'd feel like a heel. So, when I got mad, instead of saying anything to her, I'd complain, or I'd take it out on Diane and the kids. I really felt morally weak.

When I was finally able to open up and acknowledge what I was doing, I was stunned. I learned that it was easier for me to give in than to confront Frances. Once I realized this and recognized what it was doing to me and my family, I knew it was time for a change.

Diane: *I found that I was caught up in trying to pay back Frances for once saving my life. When I was a young woman on my own, I had rented a room from her in an elegant, spacious old apartment building. I got the flu, and because of my religious convictions, I was treating it only with prayer. As days passed and my condition worsened, Frances strongly advised me to see a physician she knew and trusted. I finally agreed and the doctor, after giving me medication, told Frances, "If you had not called me, Diane would not have lived until tomorrow." I had always been grateful to Frances for what she had done, and now as her caregiver, I was feeling driven to repay the favor. I couldn't allow someone to do something for me unless I could pay them back as much, or even more. I wanted to be the be-all and end-all for everyone I knew.*

Helpful Gifts

Many useful discoveries can come from honestly facing the truth about ourselves—through an inventory. Honesty is one of three gifts we can give ourselves when we start doing an inventory. Another is gentleness. When we begin to examine our feelings, thoughts, and behaviors, we need to remember that some of them have been part of us for a long time. We need to be gentle with ourselves, knowing that we developed these patterns because they made sense to us at one time. We are not bad for having them. In fact, they may have a positive side to them. They may have even helped us out many times. As we look at them, we must try to treat ourselves as lovingly as we can, keeping in mind the slogan, Easy Does It.

A third gift we can give to ourselves is forgiveness. This is discussed more in Step Five, but even as we begin our inventory, it is important to think of forgiveness—both for ourselves and the people who have wronged us.

Here's one more thing to keep in mind when doing an inventory: This is an inventory of *our* strengths and weaknesses, not anyone else's. True, we may discover in our inventory that we feel resentful or afraid because of harm others have done to us. And it's important to identify just what those feelings are, how strong they are, and who or what provoked them. In some cases, it might even mean acknowledging deeply for the first time how badly we have been treated by our parents or spouse, for example, and how much emotional pain that has caused us. All of these things can, and often do, greatly contribute to an honest and healing inventory. It is easy, however, to get sidetracked into finding fault and blaming others for our unhappiness. We may even start trying to change others.

Remember that the ultimate goal of the inventory is to bring to light *our own* feelings and actions, especially the longtime habits that either help or hinder us. From that perspective, we can change the things we can and make peace with the rest.

Most of us find an inventory to be easier and clearer when it's done in writing. Writing helps us be more specific in defining our habits, helps us sort out one concern at a time, and makes it harder to fool ourselves if we are later tempted to deny what has happened. Something about seeing our thoughts and feelings on paper makes them more vivid and acceptable.

While bearing these thoughts in mind, we can use the rest

of this chapter as a guide in writing a Fourth Step inventory.

WRITING AN INVENTORY

1. **Difficulties**

   In a journal or notebook, begin by making a list of the areas of emotional difficulty in your life, such as anger or worry, especially those related to caregiving.

2. **Causes**

   For each difficulty, list the cause(s).

3. **Barriers**

   For each difficulty, also list the barriers within yourself that may keep you from doing what you want to do about the problem. Some barriers may be ways of thinking and behaving that you developed in your childhood, ways that no longer serve you. These ways may have, in fact, become self-destructive for you. Try to see whether this is true. It helps to write them out in as much detail as possible, including how you feel about them now.

4. **Benefits**

   List the benefits to you from hanging on to each of those self-destructive ways of thinking and acting.

5. **Costs**

   Write down what each one costs you, emotionally, spiritually, or in your relationships with others. Any business owner taking an inventory will quickly get rid of items that cost the company more than benefit it. Recognizing the high cost you pay for keeping any self-destructive habits may be what finally brings you to the point where you are willing to change.

6. **Shortcomings**

   Finally, list those things you want to change. In the Twelve Step program, the things you want to change are called character defects or shortcomings. Some of them, you may not feel ready to change yet. That's all right. For now, all you have to do is make the list. Later, Steps Five through Nine will help you with the actual process of change.

In the following exercises, you will find some ideas on a few common difficulties that caregivers experience—anger, chronic grief, loneliness, fear, and worry. Write about your own experience with them. Add to the list any other difficulties you experience and write an inventory about them.

EXERCISE: ANGER

At times caregivers experience a lot of anger. You might resent the demands of caregiving and the limitations they place on you. You may even resent the illness or disability of the person you're caring for. You may resent the attitudes and actions of doctors, nurses, relatives, friends, the person you care for, God, or even yourself.

Feelings of anger and resentment are not bad. But continually hiding them or clinging to them or expressing them in hostile, harmful ways can be damaging to your serenity as well as to the serenity of those around you.

If you honestly face your anger and dig deep to examine all the causes behind it, and if you then seek some resolution to the issues by continuing with the rest of the Steps, you are on the way to finding serenity.

Causes

The causes of anger and resentment are endless. Consider these examples.

Marlene tries to be patient with her husband who has trouble moving about because of Parkinson's disease. Yet she gets impatient at times when he falls. "I yell, 'If you don't shape up, I'll ship you out!' I know better, but everybody has a breaking point."

Flora is angry that her mother can't make sensible decisions anymore. "I become completely frustrated. I want to shake her. I feel like clunking her over the head. There is just this terrific frustration at things not turning out the way I want them to."

Karen resents having to care for a mother who regarded her as property when she was a child and who still finds fault with Karen constantly. Karen trembles when she thinks about going to see her mother. "I used to shake so bad I had to take medication."

When her father lived with her, Evelyn resented her brothers and sisters who didn't call or offer to help. She also resented her father's lack of appreciation for her.

Are you also angry? What are your reasons? Write them down so you can get a full appreciation for how you feel and why you feel that way. Some caregivers find it helpful to write letters to express just how angry they are (though they may never mail them).

Barriers

What keeps you so angry? It may be something that happened years ago, and yet you may hang on tightly to your anger. You may resent the way your parents treated you and feel you can never forgive them.

You may want so much to be in control—still hesitant to surrender to your Higher Power—that you react with anger to anything that doesn't turn out the way you want.

So often caregivers feel anger even while being kind and making great sacrifices. Caregivers' anger is sometimes hidden, even from themselves. For example, Evelyn would smile pleasantly at her father every morning, although she hated having him in her house. And we in the Larsen family tried to treat Frances with courtesy even while we were seething with resentment at her manipulative ways.

The thought of admitting feelings of anger can be frightening for caregivers. You may feel so ready to explode with anger that if you ever acknowledged it, you fear losing control completely and doing something harmful. Plus, feeling anger is considered wrong, even sinful, by many people. So you hold it in.

Continue this exercise by listing your barriers to admitting your anger and letting them go.

Benefits

The "benefits" of staying angry, whether you admit it or not, can be numerous. If you don't allow yourself to express it, you can feel justified and righteous. You may think you are in control. You may think people admire you for your apparent patience. You also don't have to risk getting anger in return.

If you do explode and vent your anger on the wrong people, you may feel powerful. You may feel justified. You may intimidate others, getting your way. Others may rush to rescue you from whatever is frustrating you in order to calm or appease you.

If you are having problems with your anger, what other "benefits" do you think you may be getting? List all of them.

Costs

The biggest cost of hanging on to anger is probably your peace of mind. But physical health may also be at stake; ulcers, headaches, and backaches may signal anger simmering inside.

There are other costs as well. If you feel powerless and use your anger to feel powerful, you may remain blind to your real source—your Higher Power—and continue to feel thwarted.

At times, caregivers hang on to the anger instead of taking

action to get what they want. For example, Flora resented her children's failure to help her while she cared for two infirm people: "But I wouldn't tell them what I needed and I'd wait until I became so furious. Then I'd make demands and try to make them feel guilty, and they had no idea what I was talking about." Accumulated anger can cost healthy relationships.

What are the costs to you of staying angry? Of refusing to feel any anger at all? Of refusing to express it? Make a list of the costs you are paying.

Shortcomings

Make a list of shortcomings related to your anger. Your shortcomings may include
- blaming others
- being dishonest about feelings
- letting fear of another's anger cause you to suppress yours

Almost no one feels comfortable with anger. Take all the time you need to get to the bottom of yours. Explore, as honestly as you can, how it affects you. If you don't think you have angry feelings, pretend you do, and start over with this section of the exercise on anger. List what you *might* be angry about. Who and what would you resent? Give yourself permission to feel this emotion and learn to respect it just as you do your other emotions.

EXERCISE: CHRONIC GRIEF

Like anger, grief can be hard to express. But caregivers experience losses daily. The grief is ongoing. Sometimes it is paralyzing. Sometimes caregivers repress it.

By itself, grief is not bad. It is a normal response to loss. But it becomes troublesome if you deny it or if it becomes all-encompassing so that you cannot function.

Causes

Grief comes with every loss. Caregivers experience many losses, including the loss of

- the former relationship with the person cared for
- freedom
- time
- income
- health due to stress or overwork
- intimacy, including sexual relations
- privacy
- certainty about many things

Losing a familiar relationship with a loved one is especially hard. For example, Rita felt her mother's deteriorating condition deeply: "It felt the same as if she had died." After her mother moved into a nursing home, Rita was so depressed for a time that she couldn't face clearing out her mother's apartment. She didn't want to go through her mother's things. Finally, she moved everything to her own home where it sat for months, haunting her. When she tried to sort through it, the tears poured out. "I couldn't throw things out because Mom wasn't dead."

The grief wasn't just about her mother's belongings though. The real problem was that Rita could not recall her mother ever telling her "I love you" or showing her any affection. Rita says, "I also held back and never told her I loved her." Still, Rita had hoped that someday she and her mother might have a closer relationship. Now that her mother's mind has deteriorated, the chance is gone forever. Yet Rita is afraid to experience the grief.

If grief is a familiar feeling to you, look at the causes for your grief. Make a list of them.

Barriers

Examine ways you may be reluctant to experience grief about your losses. If you are like Rita, you may try to keep distant from grief. She even avoids telling her mother that some of her mother's friends have died, because she fears her mother may not be able to comprehend it. "I don't want to upset her," says Rita, afraid of what might follow if her mother could understand. "I don't let her cry. I fear that if she started crying, she wouldn't quit, and I wouldn't know what to do." Rita admits, after some reflection, that it is her own uncontrolled tears she is afraid of. The fear of feeling your own sadness can be a big barrier to healing your pain.

On the one hand, you may fear that you'll feel guilty if you look closely at your losses. You might blame yourself.

Shielding yourself from your losses may also be a way you're protecting yourself from the anger that is part of grief.

On the other hand, you may be very aware of your losses. You think about them a lot. Perhaps you cry often. You may seek the sympathy of others. Life may seem very unfair to you. Your way of handling your losses may be to complain about them or to withdraw. Sorrow over your losses may weigh on you endlessly.

As you write about your grief, you can discover whether you hide from it, are chronically swallowed up by it, or know how to handle it well. Make your list, based on these factors.

Benefits
    Hiding from grief may give you several "benefits" such as
- avoiding the deep pain
- admiration of others for your apparent strength
- an excuse for not assigning proper responsibility for any of the losses

Engaging in prolonged grief, especially when it becomes self-pity, may give you "benefits" too, including
- avoiding things you don't want to do
- getting attention and sympathy

- reinforcing your own beliefs about yourself, including seeing yourself as a victim who has no way to make changes

What "benefits" do you see for yourself? List them.

Costs

Hiding from your grief hides you from the truth. You may shut off part of yourself, rather than surrendering all of yourself to your Higher Power. If you are brusque, cynical, or extra busy, people may find it difficult to get close to you.

Just as with anger, you may experience some physical consequences from stuffing sad feelings.

Concentrating too much on losses takes away the possibility of joy in life. It keeps you from taking needed actions. It may suck up your energy and all your power. You can become self-centered. People may cut you off if you try to make them feel guilty and pity you.

What other costs can you see in your life? Write out all of them.

Shortcomings

List the things you want to change about yourself related to grief. Common shortcomings include
- cutting yourself off from your sad feelings
- feeling overly sorry for yourself
- being morbid
- pretending to be strong when you don't feel strong
- being a martyr

Honestly feeling grief is healthy. When you have lost someone or something important, it is proper and useful to mourn that loss. Among other things, it helps you to achieve a sense of completion about your relationship with whatever or whomever you have lost. Then you can go on with your life. The ongoing and repeated grief associated with caregiving does not give much opportunity to have that final sense of completion. The grief is likely present at some level all the time. It often feels like an open wound. If it gets no attention or care it may fester. Yet feelings about your losses can gradually heal if the grief about them gets expressed. But paying constant attention to the remaining grief leads nowhere.

You need to be very gentle with yourself regarding grief. You need to feel it when it comes up, share it with people you trust, and be willing to let it go as you are able.

EXERCISE: LONELINESS

Feeling lonely is one of the most painful emotions. Every human being has a basic need to feel connected to others. Some people who have been hurt by others try to shut out people, claiming they don't need anybody. That's the way they try to protect themselves from being hurt again. But you probably wouldn't be a caregiver if you didn't have some connection with at least one person. And that very connection puts you in a situation where you may feel less lonely.

Take a realistic look at just how much loneliness affects your life. Be honest. Allow yourself to feel compassion, as you would for another hurting person. Tears may come. That's all right. As you feel ready, go on to explore the causes.

Causes

Many caregivers feel lonely. You may spend so much time helping the person you care for and handling your other responsibilities that little time is left to be with family and friends. Even when you are with others, you may feel reluctant to talk about your concerns because you don't think anyone will understand or you may feel ashamed about something. Or you may not want to burden others. Keeping things to yourself and not feeling understood can make you feel very alone.

Some people might be uncomfortable around illness or disability and may pull back from you. You may have experienced situations where even longtime friends suddenly became too busy to see you. Such losses are hard to take.

When one spouse is caring for a disabled spouse, it may become more difficult to socialize as a couple. Even if the couple is willing to try outings or get-togethers, some friends may stop calling with invitations.

You may feel you can never leave the person you care for alone, even though you are lonely and crave other companionship. If the personality of the cared-for individual has changed, you may feel especially lonely—with no chance for an intimate relationship—let alone an ordinary conversation with the person you have counted on for years.

With these thoughts in mind, list the causes for your loneliness.

Barriers

So many of the causes of loneliness seem unavoidable. You can't change someone's health or how other people feel. Yet you can take the initiative to find companionship if that's what you want. You can share concerns with others.

Writing down answers to the following questions may help you identify barriers you may have in finding companionship.

- If you are not finding ways to reduce your loneliness, why not?
- Do you think you're unworthy? Do you think you'd be a burden?
- Are you letting your fears stop you?
- Have you taken on more than you can handle without asking for help?

- Has the withdrawal of one or two people from your life made you distrustful of others?
- Have you cut off some people because they won't help you or because they have been critical of you?
- Do you allow the person you care for to restrict your contact with others?
- What other barriers are there for you? List all of them.

Benefits

It hardly seems there are any "benefits" to loneliness. But in an unhealthy way, you may derive something from loneliness. Look more closely at the following and ask yourself if you've been getting any of these "benefits" from your loneliness.

- You don't have to deal with the problems people bring along with their companionship.
- You don't have to risk rejection or anger.
- You don't have to make an effort to find people to connect with.
- By keeping people away, you can prove true old negative beliefs you have about yourself—that you're unworthy, that you lack social skills.

What other "benefits" can you think of? Please list them.

Costs

A piece of your humanity is lost when you are isolated from others. Your thinking can become warped. You may see only one side of issues. To protect yourself, you may have cut off feelings, giving up part of yourself.

Loneliness often leads to depression, which has further costs—loss of energy and loss of self-esteem. You can lose the ability to take care of yourself and your loved one.

Loneliness may also lead you to being overtalkative or make you angry and grouchy.

There are many more costs. What is loneliness costing you? Write down your thoughts.

Shortcomings

Now make your list of the feelings, thoughts, or actions you want to change concerning loneliness. Common shortcomings are

- distrusting others
- refusing to ask for help
- feeling unworthy

None of these findings are reasons to be hard on yourself. What helps instead is to be gentle, loving, and forgiving. In Step Three you surrendered your life to the care of your Higher Power. You can trust in that care.

EXERCISE: FEAR AND WORRY

When someone you love is chronically ill or disabled, it feels like things are always going wrong. The mistake the nurse made yesterday, the important papers that were misplaced last week, or the nasty family fight last year still haunts you. Tomorrow promises more uncertainty about the medicine, the progress of the disease, or the living arrangements. The phone might ring at any moment with more bad news. With all these concerns, you may easily get swallowed up in fear and worry.

Causes

This list will probably be easy to develop. Caregivers are susceptible to a host of worries, such as

- fear of more health complications
- fear of the loss of physical or mental capabilities
- fear of job and income loss

- worry about the pain of a loved one
- worry about doctor appointments, medications, side effects, and treatment outcomes
- fear that things won't be done right if someone else does them

So many troublesome questions can come to the mind of caregivers, including

- Am I doing the right thing?
- Will everybody fulfill their promises?
- What happens if I get ill or lose my job or abilities?
- Will I be able to take a vacation or go to school or follow through on my other plans?
- What should I do about that unsettled matter from yesterday or last week?
- What can I do to get the person I care for to take the medicine, be less angry or violent, stop complaining, and feel better?
- Am I doing enough?

The uncertainty, the pain, the inability to do enough—all such concerns can induce worry.

Many causes for fear and worry have already been listed. Include any that apply to you in your list, and add others that affect you.

Barriers

If you surrender your will and your life to the care of your Higher Power, you can release your fears and worries as soon as they appear. So what stops you?

One answer is—more fear. You may be afraid to give up control. You may fear that if you don't worry, something bad will happen. But when you do worry, you may still fear something bad will happen. This is all evidence of powerlessness and the "insanity" talked about in the first two Steps. You can get in such a swirl of fear and worry that, at times, you end up in full-fledged panic.

The opposite of fear is trust. Being unwilling to trust is another barrier you may be familiar with. If you were hurt badly by your parents or others early in life, you may think that bad things are inevitable. You may constantly expect them. Avoid being hard on yourself if you feel this way. It was probably a way you learned as a powerless child to alert yourself to dangers around you. You probably even learned not to trust *yourself*.

You can yet learn to relax and trust, to believe in yourself, in others, and in God. Following the Twelve Steps is a good way to begin that process.

List your barriers to letting go of fear and worry.

Benefits

There are no *real* benefits to staying fearful and worried. Yet you might twist your thinking to believe there are some advantages.

- By being fearful, you can become overly cautious and not take risks. You can have an illusion that you are safe, even though you don't feel very safe.
- By not trusting, you may think you can keep yourself from being hurt.
- You may think worry keeps trouble away.
- Worry can give you something to focus on when you don't have any control.

Are you getting some "benefits" from being fearful and worrying? Make your list.

Costs

If your fears keep you from acting and taking risks that

could be helpful, you play it safe and don't really experience life. You are too busy living in the past or the future to ever appreciate what is happening here and now. Because of this, you miss many of the simple joys of life—the brightness in someone's eyes or the gift of another's "thank you" that you take for granted.

Worrying is exhausting. It can drain you of energy that could be used to solve problems or to live in gratitude. You may worry so much about the people you care for that you never spend time just *being* with them, learning what they have noticed about the movement of sunlight across the room or listening with them to the early morning birdsongs.

Fear and worry are ways to avoid other feelings. You can cover up anger or grief with worry.

List the costs to you of your worrying or fearfulness.

Shortcomings
List what you want to change about your fearfulness and worrying. Common shortcomings related to fear are
- lacking trust in others
- nagging
- playing it safe
- being joyless

You can't eliminate worry completely. You may never be able to totally calm your fears. You have many things to keep track of, and plan for, and account for. Some may be very confusing, demanding, and frightening. Some things will, in fact, get worse.

But little by little, the Twelve Steps can help you release your worries, shed your fears, and expand your ability to trust. As you do so, you will be able to see that no amount of fear and worry changes anything. A tense stomach and tight, wrinkled brow aren't very likely to give you peace of mind.

Only when you accept what you can't control, and act to change what you can, will peace of mind come about.

But you must be patient and loving with yourself along the way, maybe even laughing at yourself a little if you find yourself fretting needlessly. Some days, the best you may be able to do is just acknowledge that you are worried. Over time, by working the Twelve Steps, you can learn more and more how to Let Go and Let God.

Other Problem Areas

The preceding exercises included an inventory of anger, chronic grief, loneliness, fear, and worry. But these are just *some* of the difficulties we experience as caregivers. We can use the same procedure for other problems. Perhaps we get people to do things our way by trying to make them feel guilty or by sulking. We could do an inventory under the category *control*. Perhaps we are so responsible for others that we have given away a big piece of ourselves. Examples of this are making decisions for others when they can make their own, or apologizing for someone else's behavior as if we were to blame. Inappropriately taking responsibility for others in this way is called *caretaking,* and it is another possible topic for an inventory. Some other common problems for caregivers are embarrassment, jealousy, guilt, perfectionism, and exhaustion.

List Your Positive Qualities Too

To balance our inventories, we also examine our strengths as caregivers. Our patience, faithfulness, willingness to learn new things, sense of humor, and other positive qualities probably contribute to our ability to care for someone as well as to maintain our own well-being. List all of these on paper.

We can pat ourselves on the back for the positive ways in which we have handled ourselves with respect to each of the difficulties we've considered.

After completing an inventory, we have a much better understanding of our life. We can see more clearly how our habits direct so many of our feelings, thoughts, and actions. This may be the first time we have thoroughly examined these habits—both those that help and those that hinder. We may have cleared up some things that have puzzled us for a long time. Some of this may be hard to take in. Fortunately, the next Steps can teach us what to do with these discoveries and the discomfort they may cause.

Remember, we have been able to do this because we have placed our trust in our Higher Power. We can continue that act of surrender now as we go on to Step Five and share what we have discovered.

Chapter 5

Giving Away the Pain

STEP FIVE: Admitted to God, to ourselves, and to another
human being the exact nature of our wrongs.

Having explored our strengths and weaknesses through a
Step Four inventory, we have moved a long way down the
path of honesty. We have allowed ourselves, perhaps for the
first time, to look closely at how we live our life. We have had
an opportunity to identify the difficulties we face, to learn
what causes them, and to examine how we respond to them.
To do this has likely taken great courage.

In the process of doing a moral inventory, our ego may
have become deflated. We caregivers often try to look good
at all times, even to ourselves, and our inventory may show
what was hiding behind our "looking good." Naturally,
our ego may try to get us back to looking good as fast as
possible. If we feel ashamed, we'll want to move away from
that feeling. We may see the need for many changes and feel
the job is just too big. Or we may feel defiant, tending to
downplay our defects, trying to justify our harmful behavior
by emphasizing how hard our life is. Or we may decide we
are too busy to bother with all this. Another ego response is

to blame someone else for our problems and behaviors, with thoughts such as, *I haven't done anything so wrong; look at what he's done. Now there is somebody who really needs to do an inventory.*

To help prevent us from getting trapped in our narrow ego's perspective, the program offers us Step Five as a way to reinforce the honesty of Step Four. We are advised to admit our "wrongs" to ourselves, to God, and to another human being.

At this point, we can recognize the wisdom of writing down our *strengths* as well as our weaknesses, as suggested in Step Four. We will need to draw on these strengths to move through Step Five. Step Five takes courage, but it is the same courage that was required of us in working the previous Steps, as well as the courage we practice daily in our role as caregivers. Mostly likely, we have handled difficult matters and taken considerable risks on behalf of the people we care for. We can call on that same courage to support our commitment to our own growth and healing. If we falter, we can count on our Higher Power to supply everything we need.

The Benefits

Although Step Five takes courage, it also provides many benefits. It gives us a direct way to share our pain and accept responsibility for our actions. Much of our pain has been hard to admit. We may have tried to hide how angry or jealous or embarrassed we have felt over some things that have happened. We want people to think we have everything under control or that we only think and do "good" things. We do not want others to know the full truth about us. Yet, we want them to love us as we are.

How can anyone love us as we are if we don't let them know *who* we are? Can we even love ourselves if we haven't faced the truth about ourselves? The Fifth Step asks us to admit our shortcomings not once, but three times, so we can no longer hide out in the false protection of dishonesty. By stating them over and over, we come to accept our feelings—all of them. We quit trying to justify our actions. We see clearly how we contribute to the problems in our life, whether in small or large ways.

Without taking Step Five, we can stay in the world of pretend, and our problems will get worse. We're like the person who inevitably trips over the broken front step long in need of repair. Better to call attention to the problem and make plans to fix the steps.

> **Diane:** *When Frances was living with us, I was in a mono-lithic state of denial. She was manipulative. She even lied. Frances exercised a form of tyranny over me, and I felt I had no path of recourse. It was as if I had an immovable, nonpenetrable piece of steel straight up and down my body. I denied anything was wrong.*
>
> *Only when I broke down and told an understanding geriatric social worker how powerless I felt and how much I resented Frances did things begin to change. This wonderful social worker was so compassionate. She listened, she acknowledged my feelings, and she seemed to really understand. I felt released from my state of denial. I could begin to take steps to solve the problem.*

Often, we caregivers are reluctant to tell the truth about ourselves because we think others will be repelled by it. Instead, what many of us find when we share our Fifth Step with another person is a great deal of understanding and acceptance. Someone who knows the meaning of a Fifth Step will usually listen with great love and compassion. (On pages 70–74, we discuss how to choose someone to hear our Fifth Step.) All of the feelings we have had are common human

SELF-CARE *for* CAREGIVERS

feelings, and this listener will probably let us know some ways he or she has also experienced these feelings at times. Many people feel a great sense of relief to at last find someone who understands, someone who sees his or her flaws as a normal part of being human. Then our terrible secrets lose some of their magnitude. The deep sense of shame is lifted.

> **Diane:** *From talking to the social worker, I got a new perspective. I learned I didn't have to put up with that stuff from Frances anymore.*

Getting an added perspective often happens when sharing a Fifth Step. To us, alone, the view of our circumstances and ourselves is often limited, even when we have tried to be honest in our inventory. By sharing our inventory with another person, we may get feedback that clears away some long-bothersome haze. We may get the encouragement we need to act on decisions we have hesitated to carry out. Our listener may help us find the courage to forgive ourselves.

Learning about forgiveness is a benefit of the Fifth Step. So much is expected of us as caregivers that we may often feel we fall short. We become hard on ourselves. In the Fifth Step, by bringing our shortcomings out into the open and sharing them with God and another caring person, we start to experience forgiveness. Like loosening a belt notched too tight for too long, the Fifth Step relieves the constricting pressure of our guilt. We may even find that some of our troubles came from our taking on needless blame and guilt. We may realize that we felt ashamed about the laziness, the rudeness, or mistakes of our spouse, our relatives, or the person we care for—actions and attitudes that were not our fault. We see how much harm we have done to ourselves.

We also see how much our denial has hurt us, how very hard it is to acknowledge our pain and our genuine wrongdoings. As we make these discoveries, we can feel compassion toward others who may have character defects like ours. As we find the humility that comes in working the Fifth Step, we can begin to forgive ourselves and others. We may realize, too, that we can't wish away or force away our defects by ourselves.

One of the greatest benefits from sharing our Fifth Step with someone else is a sense of connection, of belonging to the human family. We can finally be drawn out of our isolation and loneliness. We can begin to trust someone else, something that may be difficult for us if we are used to handling everything by ourselves. If we can trust one person with the truth about ourselves, maybe we can trust others. We don't have to feel so alone. We don't have to take all the responsibility for things. We can ask for help. We can set limits on what we will do for others, and limits on what we will allow others to do to us.

Taking an inventory helps business owners know how much they are worth. Taking our own personal inventory does the same for us in our Fourth Step. We know our traits that help us; we know those traits that hurt us. In our Fifth Step, we learn that our self-worth does not depend on what we do or don't do. Rather, we can always be forgiven. Our value is in just being ourselves.

Acknowledging to God

Working all three parts of Step Five is important. We begin by turning to God.

One misconception many caregivers have is thinking we can go it alone. The first part of Step Five—admitting our wrongs to our Higher Power—helps us over that barrier. In Step Three, we agreed to surrender our will and our life to the God of our understanding. To do this likely took an enormous act of trust. Since we have taken that Step, we can turn now to our Higher Power and surrender a part of our life that we now know more about—our shortcomings.

If our Higher Power is God, we may think God already knows these things and wonder why it's necessary to say them again. The purpose of this part of the Fifth Step is not to report something unknown to God. Rather, we are *admitting* to our faults. Having accepted them, we bring them to God and look for further acceptance and forgiveness.

Acknowledging to Ourselves

Second, we turn inward, acknowledging to *ourselves* all we discovered in Step Four as ours. This may be as simple as reviewing the exercises we have written for Step Four. Sometimes, in taking a fresh look at this writing, even more information surfaces. If the writing is somewhat disorganized, we use Step Five to make sure we clearly identify our character defects that need attention. It's a good idea to write this list separately and keep it handy as we work the Steps that follow. It can help us to remember what we discovered, especially if we start slipping into denial. Some people choose to destroy their Step Four writings after completing the Fifth Step to symbolize a fresh start. By having a separate list of our defects, we are less likely to get rid of that along with the rest of our inventory—which might be tempting. It would be easy to think that once we had uncovered our bad habits, we wouldn't go back to them anymore. The Twelve Step program, however, is not a quick-fix program. We have seven more Steps to take in the process of our healing and growth. And some of our habits may take a very long time to change.

Acknowledging to Another Person

Now, for the third part of Step Five, we reach out again, to another human being. We admit our wrongs to a person we trust.

Selecting the right person is very important. We can share our entire inventory with one person, or we can choose to reveal part of it to one person and the rest to another. We look for someone we are willing to trust. It can be someone very close to us, or a person who can be more objective. Some people turn to a member of the clergy, a therapist, or some other professional. If at all possible, it's best to select someone who understands the Twelve Steps and fully appreciates how important this conversation is to us. By all means, the person should be someone we are certain will hold whatever we say in complete confidence.

We may be reluctant to ask someone for fear we will be turned down or thought less of. But most often, people are honored to be asked and appreciate the trust placed in them. We must be careful that our fears don't keep us from working this important part of the Step.

Whomever we choose, we should keep in mind that the purpose of the Fifth Step is self-disclosure for our healing and growth. We must choose someone who will help us achieve that purpose.

Once we make the selection, we can ask if the person is willing to hear our Fifth Step, and set a time and place where we can be free of interruptions. How the meeting is structured is up to us. The only necessary ingredient is that we share our findings from our inventory. Some people read aloud what they have written. What's more important is being honest. If possible, we use this time to fully express some of our deepest feelings. It may be one of the few times when we have the opportunity to feel safe with someone who is prepared to be an attentive listener to us. This is a very rich opportunity.

We can ask the listener for feedback to help us be as honest as possible and to open the way for forgiveness and change. For example, if we are taking full blame for everything that went wrong in some situation, the listener might suggest that we claim only our own shortcomings and not take on responsibility for the actions of others. Or, if we are speaking harshly of someone and fail to acknowledge our own wrongdoings in a troubled relationship, the listener might gently ask us to look beyond the immediate frustration to see why we are holding on to that resentment. We should try not to be defensive. If advice is offered, we are free to accept or reject it. We can ask for guidance from our Higher Power on this. The goal in this Step is simply acknowledgment of our wrongs. Once we complete our Fifth Step, we can turn everything over to our Higher Power. We needn't worry whether we did it "right." We need only be sincere and do our best.

The Fifth Step is a cherished practice and often a turning point in the Twelve Step program. Many people experience a great sense of relief through it, a new sense of connection with their Higher Power and with others, a new sense of freedom. Most important, it is a chance to become clear and honest about our past and present life. Now that we've acknowledged the source of our difficulties and the wrongs we have done, we can begin to clear away harmful or useless thoughts and behaviors; we can create a more satisfying future for ourselves.

Two reasons that people hesitate to do the Fifth Step are difficulty in choosing a listener and fear of exposing the negative side of themselves. Following are two exercises that can help in getting past these barriers.

EXERCISE: CHOOSING A LISTENER

Make a list of people you trust at least a little. Include relatives, friends, professionals, acquaintances you admire, and so forth.

Plan to spend a quiet time away from interruptions to consider your list. During this time, begin with a prayer asking for your Higher Power's guidance. Go down your list quickly, crossing off names of people you are quite certain are not appropriate for your Fifth Step. From the rest, narrow the list to three or four names—people who understand the Twelve Steps or who at least would be willing to give you an understanding ear and keep a confidence. Again, ask your Higher Power for guidance. If no one name stands out, close your eyes for a few moments and relax. Picture yourself in a life-threatening situation. Consider the people left on your list. Who would you call first? Who would you trust to help you out? If you could trust your *life* to this person when you want someone to save your life, perhaps he or she is worthy of your trust concerning *how* you live your life.

Remember, you aren't going to find a perfect person. In fact, you wouldn't want to. Make your choice based on your best judgment after asking for guidance, and trust the outcome to your Higher Power.

If you prefer to talk to someone you don't know, consider selecting a professional recommended by people you trust. Ask friends about their experience with counselors, clergy, and retreat directors. You can contact recommended individuals and tell them what you want. Find out how familiar they are with Fifth Steps. Ask them what you could expect if you chose them. Ask them if they charge a fee or request a donation. Again, count on your Higher Power's guidance to help you find an appropriate person.

EXERCISE: WORKING THROUGH THE FEAR

If you are fearful of exposing your faults to someone else, here are some activities that might help you.

- Review the section on fear and worry in Chapter Four. Also review your answers to the exercises in that section.
- Imagine that someone you love is in your situation and

feels as you do. Write that person a letter, lovingly offering encouragement to go ahead with the Fifth Step. Acknowledge his or her fears, and offer all the ideas you can think of that would help that person be able to proceed. Write it as if that person's life and happiness depended on this letter. After you have finished, set the letter aside for a few days. Then, re-read the letter as if it were addressed to you. The letter was written in love, expressing your own internal wisdom. Receive it in love, trust your own wisdom, and act on it.

- In a quiet time, preferably after dark, and when you can be by yourself, light a candle. Turn out all other lights. Focus on the candle and enjoy its beauty. Enjoy the dancing of the flame. Notice how much light the little flame gives off. Notice how it fills the room, fills your soul. Imagine that the wax is made up of your fears. Watch them melt away. Feel them melt away within yourself. Let the light represent love and forgiveness. Let love and forgiveness fill the room, fill your soul. Now imagine the person who will receive your Fifth Step. Imagine that person filled with love and forgiveness, offering it to you. Willingly accept these gifts. Now make plans to receive them by contacting this person to set a time for your Fifth Step meeting.

STEP SIX: Were entirely ready to have God remove all our defects of character.

If anyone asked if we would like all our pain and our defects removed, our quick reply would likely be, "Of course." Particularly if we have done a thorough job of compiling and revealing our inventory, we may be squirming a bit, ill at ease with some of the troublesome things we have uncovered. We would just as soon be rid of them all. So does that mean we are all set to have God remove them? Are we "entirely ready"?

Readiness is a state of ripeness. Think of a wheat field standing tall with golden shafts ripened by the sun. The grain is harvested and then transformed through milling and baking into wonderful, nourishing food. Step Six invites us to stand ready for a harvest, to let God shake loose the chaff and use the golden kernels that remain to produce something rich and valuable.

But are we ready? How willing are we to be transformed? How prepared are we to have our longtime habits shaken loose? Step Six calls for a deepening of the surrender we experienced in Step Three. We are to give God complete charge of our life so that we produce what is rich and valuable.

We might think that we will have no trouble letting go of our difficulties—the loneliness, the anger, the fear, and the rest of the emotional pain we explored in Step Four. But we also found during our inventory that there are some "benefits" to hanging on to those difficulties. Loneliness and isolation protect us from having to deal with people. Anger justifies our feeling superior. Fear keeps us "safe."

Besides, day by day, hour by hour, we are confronted with so many aggravations that may provoke negative reactions. We may want to be kind and forgiving. But when the person we care for *demands* rather than *asks* that we prepare a meal, or puts shoes on the wrong feet, or repeatedly refuses necessary medication, our anger may break loose despite our best intentions. We want to have trust, but fear can creep into our consciousness every time we see another possible accident, a turn for the worse, or another loss.

With all these aggravations, problems, and potential problems tugging at us, we often react instinctively, out of habit. We may panic. We might want someone to blame, maybe even ourselves. We may try to take over. We often feel so responsible for how things turn out. We try to be on the spot to make sure everything is done the right way.

Or maybe we react differently—we may be the kind of person who pulls back when uncomfortable situations arise. Our motto may be "I'm too busy" or "I don't know how this is done" if we're asked to unscramble the medical bills and insurance forms or confront a relative who is taking advantage of the disabled person. We may only take action when there is no chance of a mistake or a controversy.

When we are under pressure, some of our worst habits surface and demand center stage. Then, feeling guilty or embarrassed, we try very hard to hold them back. If we can't control things around us, we at least try to keep our feelings and behaviors under control. Or we may turn to alcohol or food or television or some other handy comfort to try to suppress or hide out from our feelings and reactions.

No wonder *insanity* is talked about in Step Two. The circumstances surrounding caregiving can create an environment that feels crazy and unmanageable. And the more we try to get control of the situation and our feelings and behavior, the crazier we feel. Our defects pop up everywhere. But we may not always be ready to admit to them. Denial quickly kicks in when, already feeling that the affairs of caregiving are more than we can handle, we are asked to also fix what's wrong with ourselves.

Even all our work from Steps Four and Five can slip into the background amidst the day-to-day strains of living. Yet, here is Step Six, asking us to get ready to have God remove our defects. At this point, we may feel like throwing in the towel. How can we be asked to find the energy to begin making big changes in our life with all we have to deal with already?

Leaving It to Your Higher Power

If that is our thinking, we can be reassured. Step Six already assumes that we have tried to change our ways. If we had been able to leave behind all the emotional pain and all our ineffective strategies for dealing with it, we would have done so. That's why Step Six doesn't ask us to make changes. It only asks that we be entirely ready to have our Higher Power make these changes. That should be a relief, and it is, in a way. But still, we are reluctant. Why?

The hardest part of change is the feeling that, if we change, we won't be the same. We are afraid of change, because change means leaving behind something familiar and, instead, embracing the unfamiliar. Change fills us with uncertainty. If we change, what will we have to give up? What will we find in its place? What will be left of us? What will we discover hiding behind what we give up?

Considering these questions is part of the process of working Step Six. We can think about them, write about them, pray about them. As we do, we get in touch with our reluctance to change. We see how we cling to our old ways because they are so familiar, so predictable. Even the misery they cause us becomes predictable. We can find some comfort in knowing what to expect. Our familiar ways may also protect us from the feelings we have been hiding underneath our behaviors. We may always take control because under-neath we are afraid to trust anyone else. Or we may give in, not out of generosity or kindness, but because we are so afraid of someone else's wrath or judgment about us. So often, it is our fears that hide beneath our self-destructive ways. We may be afraid of what faces us because we don't think we can handle whatever it is.

Step Six, then, asks us to exhibit great courage. We are asked to assume a state of readiness and receptivity to the guidance of our Higher Power. Like the stalk of wheat, we are to become vulnerable to the wind and rain of life, as well as the sunshine. We are to risk, in the end, giving up the flimsy stalk of our self-will that does not hold us up well in stormy times. Finally, when we are ready for the harvest, we release ourselves from our self-will, surrendering to our Higher Power the "self" we have held up so high. We then become transformed like the wheat through the daily grinding and mixing and kneading and heating of our life.

When this happens, something new and priceless will emerge from behind all our fears, worries, and insanity. We find our deeper purpose. We find peace of mind. We become comfortable with being an instrument of God's will, offering service to the world and those around us, not out of guilt or duty or fear, but out of a deep love and joy, deeper than we have ever known before.

Ways of Becoming Ready

How can we possibly get to such a place of surrender and openness, to become willing to be transformed this profoundly? One thing is certain: we can't rush the process. Just as the wheat takes time to ripen, so do we. We may need many nudges before we make ourselves ready. Denying problems and resisting change are strong instincts. The problems may have to grow larger and become more threatening to bring us to maturity. We don't often make changes until the pain of doing things the old way becomes too much to bear. It may take waiting until things get that bad before we can actually surrender into a state of readiness.

But some caregivers use other ways to prepare themselves.

First of all, working the first five Steps is the best preparation there is. We have already looked at the notion of surrender once before, in Step Three. We have also had an opportunity to survey our weaknesses and be willing to acknowledge them to others. This is the primary path of preparation. But, if we are still reluctant, we can ready ourselves in other ways.

Marvin: I was reluctant to have anything change. But I've

come to a place of accepting that I'm changing all the time anyhow. So, if a particular change is good for me, I figure, Why not? To get to that point, though, I have to begin with a lot of opening myself up.

Diane: *I had to get quiet and really listen. One thing that really helped was watching Frances change. When we used to go visit her at the high-rise, she would always try to make us feel guilty when we left. She would say, "Why don't you stay longer?" and "Do you have to leave me alone?" But in her final years, her outlook changed. Even though her health was failing, she would smile and say, "It does no good to complain," and she would take my hand and say, "I have so many wonderful memories of our time together." I saw that even at age ninety, people can change. That was a real gift to me.*

Other Ways of Becoming Ready

Rita found she had to be patient with herself. "I wasn't willing for a long time. I didn't want to give up my resentments and my anger."

Flora says she spends a lot of time on Step Six. "I don't know if the outcome is always as successful as I'd like." She says her self-will gets in the way. But she tries to help bring herself to a state of readiness during prayer by placing her hands in an open posture, exhibiting a receptivity to God's will.

An Ongoing Process

Being ready is not a one-time thing. We must continually bring ourselves back to this state because our reluctance will surface again and again. Our self-will is at work trying to protect the status quo. Each time we renew our efforts to become ready, it's easy to get impatient with ourselves, and with our Higher Power. We become annoyed with ourselves when we repeat old, ineffective behaviors long after we were ready to be rid of them. We get mad at our Higher Power for not taking them away. This impatience is another sign of our trying to be in control. Our self-will takes over: we want to decide what character defects will be removed, and when. But Step Six only asks us to get ready, entirely ready.

Maybe we never reach an ideal state of being "entirely" ready. We may want to hold on to some of our old ways. We may also believe that we know better than our Higher Power what we need. But each time we approach Step Six, we are given another opportunity to examine how ready we are and to see what we have left to surrender. We become as ready as we can be at that particular time and then go on to Step Seven.

EXERCISE: GETTING READY

To get a better sense of what readiness means, make a list of five to ten things that illustrate being ready. Here are some examples: being ready for a performance to start, being dressed up for some activity, having the food set out just before a meal, having warmed up before a game. For each item on your list, consider the following.

- what it takes to become ready
- what must be given up
- how much change must take place
- the possible results
- whether it will be worth it
- what will happen if a state of readiness is not reached

Now pick one item from your readiness list and imagine yourself in that particular state of readiness. Try to see and feel the experience as vividly as you can. Now slowly go through the above considerations, this time noticing how you personally experience all the implications of being ready. Write a paragraph or more about what you experience.

Now look at the list of character defects from your inventory and imagine yourself ready to give them up. Do the same exercise with each item on this list, considering deeply the specific implications of letting go of that defect.

STEP SEVEN: Humbly asked God to remove our shortcomings.

Now that we have become ready to have our character defects removed, we ask our Higher Power to remove them. And we ask this with humility. It sounds like a simple act at first—a straightforward request. Yet, what we are asking for is a complete process of transformation to take place. Where we have been impatient, we ask for patience. Where we have been stagnated by fear, we ask for courage to take action. Where we have worried day and night, we ask to be freed from worries. And so on.

When the magnitude of what we are asking for becomes apparent, we might find ourselves stopping for a moment to question whether this is even possible. Can we really change that dramatically? Why would our Higher Power be bothered with such a request? Perhaps it is rather presumptuous to expect a response. Are we worthy?

Yet Step Seven states our task quite clearly—asking our Higher Power to "remove our shortcomings"—with the implied assumption that the request will be granted. The only qualifier is that we do it humbly. If what we ask for is great in this Step, so is what is asked of us. Making such a sizable request requires sizable faith. To get the results we want, we are asking our Higher Power to be totally in charge. We are not offering some sort of bargain—I'll do some and you do some. We are not mapping out our strategy for change and hoping our Higher Power will help out a little. We are asking that our Higher Power be responsible for the complete removal of our shortcomings. We are daring to turn over to our Higher Power this seemingly monumental task that we have unsuccessfully tried to do ourselves for years. We are giving up being in charge.

Humility

To have such bold faith takes humility. For many of us, humility is the cornerstone of a Twelve Step program, and nowhere is it more essential than in the Seventh Step. No shortcomings will be removed, nothing will change, unless we approach this Step humbly.

The notion of being humble may leave us uncomfortable at first. We might abhor humility, feeling it is a weakness and an obstacle to getting things done. Perhaps we're used to being in charge. We may see ourselves as decisive, confident, efficient. Humility doesn't seem to fit; we see what we want and we go after it. Why is it then that we oftentimes feel lonely, simmer with rage, or feel powerless over so many things in our role as caregivers? Despite our aggressive, go-for-it way of operating, we're often left with a list of difficulties and character defects that haunt us.

Perhaps some of us reject being humble because in humility lies the truth, and the truth hurts. The truth is, for all our efficiency, that we can't cure the infirmities of our loved ones. We can't make them change how they act. Many of us are so used to storming through life, taking charge, getting things done. But we have had little practice with humility—standing in the face of what is, and knowing that ultimately we can't control it.

Humility asks self-will to resign from power. It does not belittle us. It is not a sign of weakness, but strength. A humble person is strong—strong enough to recognize and respond to the truth. Humility means acknowledging our strengths and weaknesses with complete honesty, and putting them all into the service of the Higher Power that keeps order and balance around us. It means letting go of those desires and plans that are narrow and selfish. It means opening ourselves to fulfilling our larger purpose in life.

Some of us may be repelled by the notion of being humble for a very different reason. We may have spent our life "eating humble pie." We may have given in to others, let others run over us. We may have had our fill of humility. But lowering and discounting ourselves are no more signs of humility than a take-charge, know-it-all attitude.

Whether we resist being humble by seeing ourselves as less than we are, or by appearing to be more than we are, neither approach recognizes the truth about ourselves. Humility is seeing and living by our true nature to the best of our ability.

Many of us thought we had to be self-reliant to make it in the world. We may be great at striving for success, striving to improve. When things weren't working out, we sometimes turned to our Higher Power as a last resort, hoping to be rescued. Then, if that didn't work, we got angry at our Higher Power or decided we weren't worthy of our Higher Power's help.

With humility, we come to rely on our Higher Power *first*. We see that our role is to carry out our Higher Power's plan, not to enlist our Higher Power in carrying out ours.

Staying Humble

We often get so absorbed in our goals, trying harder and harder to achieve them when we meet with obstacles. The same thing can happen with Step Seven. At times, we forget what this Step says, and we start working hard at removing our shortcomings ourselves. Or we ask our Higher Power to do the job, but then we keep a checklist to see how well it's going. If the shortcomings aren't removed on our timetable, we may get frustrated. Once again, we have taken charge.

Each time we realize that we've slipped into our self-centered, controlling ways, we can remind ourselves of our need for humility. With humility, we ask, not demand, that our Higher Power remove our shortcomings. We let our Higher Power decide when and how this happens. If we still experience some of our defects, we can ask ourselves whether we have done all we can to become entirely ready to have them removed. If we have, then we can remember that God knows better than we do what our defects are and is removing them in a way that is best for us. With humility, we can express gratitude as we notice what is changing for the better. We can be satisfied with improvement, rather than perfection. Maybe we can even learn to laugh at ourselves when we become impatient with our Higher Power for not removing our impatience, or angry at our Higher Power because we're still so angry.

Rita's Story

Rita had lived by herself for years. She liked her independence, but she welcomed her parents when they came for short visits after their retirement. Gradually though, the visits began to last several weeks, then several months. After her father died, Rita's mother spent six months of the year at her daughter's house.

Slowly, deep and long-held resentments began to surface. Rita was angry that, throughout her life, her mother had never shown her any sign of love, never offered a word of encouragement or praise. Yet, she tried to be nice to her mother anyway—out of a sense of duty.

But her fury grew as the lengthy and unwelcome visits continued year after year. She became obsessed with her anger. She gained weight. She smoked heavily. She could hardly concentrate on her work. Even after fourteen years of these visits, Rita was afraid to tell her mother how she felt. She feared further alienation from her mother.

"I found myself complaining over and over to my friends about my mother's visits." Among her Twelve Step friends, she found some good and caring listeners. "Finally, one of them gave me the kick in the butt I needed, and I started seeing a psychologist. The psychologist recommended that I tell my mother not to stay with me anymore. It took me a long time, but I finally wrote a letter to my mother and told her how I felt, without blaming her or criticizing her. Mom didn't make it easy. She wrote back saying she didn't realize what a burden she had been, blaming herself. I felt even more guilty and more angry. But the psychologist and my Twelve Step friends helped me to work through a lot of those feelings."

Rita helped her mother find an apartment of her own. But within a year, she began to notice that her mother was unable to make ordinary decisions, even to write checks. She noticed bruises on her mother and became alarmed when her mother fell while getting dressed and broke her arm. Before long, the doctor recommended placing her mother in a nursing home.

Rita's guilt resurfaced quickly. She blamed herself for her mother's condition. She was angry at herself for not noticing sooner her mother's difficulties. She was also angry that, having finally freed herself from the burden of her mother's visits, she now had the new burden of overseeing health care for her mother. All of this anger created more guilt—about being angry.

The new responsibility brought with it even more duties, adding to Rita's swirl of obsessive feelings. She had to clear out her mother's apartment and decide what to do with her belongings. She had to handle legal, financial, and medical matters. And then there were the frequent visits to the nursing home. The worry, the anger, the grief, the shame, the exhaustion pressed in on Rita. "At times, I felt there was so much on my shoulders. I would be so frustrated. But then I knew I didn't have to rely on just my own strength."

She turned to the Twelve Steps. With humility, she called on her Higher Power for help. "A lot has been released. I've given up some of my resentments and anger. I don't carry around the guilt now. I realize this is the way things are, and I can't go back." She has even begun giving her mother hugs, though Rita grew up without any.

At times, she still worries. "I have to handle her finances. It's hard figuring out the hospital bills and who's supposed to pay what. There's the insurance, and then there's Medicare and Social Security. Sometimes I worry that I can't handle it. I say to myself, *I've got to do this and I've got to do that.* But then I say, *No, I can't do it all today. I'll handle some of it tomorrow; and if I can't do it, worrying won't help.*

When Rita feels sorry for herself, wondering why she is stuck with all this, she calls her brothers and sisters who live in other cities, and they are very supportive.

At times, she sinks back into her old self-defeating thinking. "Nothing my mother says makes any sense anymore, and I know that, but I was really thrown off center one day near Christmas when I visited her."

Rita had decided to enjoy Christmas day with some out-of-town friends, rather than with her mother. Small surges of guilt would seize her from time to time as Christmas approached, but she did her best to dismiss them. She decided to visit her mother two days before Christmas, and she dreaded going: she knew the guilt would be pushing itself into her consciousness again. But she also knew she had to go. During the visit, she just sat with her mother and tried to show some interest in the stream of nonsense talk that had now become so familiar. "All of a sudden," Rita recalls, "Mom blurted out, 'It's all your fault.' Guilt just grabbed hold of me. I started to shake. I felt so powerless. I couldn't help myself. I believed she meant it. I was upset for days.

"But my Twelve Step friends helped me. They reminded me that she doesn't mean anything she says now. And even if she did, I can't control her feelings. I prayed a lot to my Higher Power, asking for help to control my feelings."

Rita knows she has improved because she doesn't let her painful feelings stay with her and make her tense and depressed for long periods as they used to. Still, her mother is very much on her mind every day. She knows she must work her program One Day at a Time, continually asking her Higher Power to remove her shortcomings. But she still has trouble releasing some of them. "The big one now is procrastination. I beat myself up over that. I am willing to have it removed, but I haven't asked my Higher Power yet. I believe that when I become really willing, it will be removed quickly."

A Time of Healing

Becoming willing and humbly asking our Higher Power are the two Steps that relieve us of our agonizing emotional pain and our ineffective attempts to control what we cannot control. Flora describes the process as "handing over my ego for a tune-up and being open." When she does that, she says, "Some kind of healing happens. I find myself in a posture with my hands open and I wait to see what's put into them. I usually see light put into them." The light is an image that helps her experience the healing of her pain. She also describes images of "clearing away the scales," "scraping off rough sandburs," "rubbing off rough, dry skin," and "anointing with oil."

However we identify our Higher Power, we can experience this healing. We may feel a void or some rawness as our character defects are removed. We have to be willing to stand in that place of discomfort for a time. Every change requires some adjustment. Mostly we experience a sense of release.

> *Marvin: I prayed for a long time for Frances to change, and then for myself to change. But I realized I could let go of the problem and nobody has to change. Once I let go and let God provide me with a different attitude, I could tell Frances no, without feeling guilty, and still respect her dignity and my own.*

Respecting our dignity and that of others is at the heart of humility. If we as caregivers recognize our full dignity, we know that we deserve a life of sanity, serenity, and fulfillment. When we are willing to turn our life over to God, we can have this kind of life. We become more willing to embrace what is, and less likely to complain or agonize over what isn't going the way our ego wants. We see that what our Higher Power has in mind for us is best. We give up our pursuit of anything else.

EXERCISE: A VISUALIZATION

Sit quietly by yourself and close your eyes. Relax your body and welcome into your mind the image of a warm waterfall washing over you in a beautiful forest, cleansing away the sweat and dirt accumulated from your travels. Imagine the soothing, clean feeling of the water. Then, as you stand in the warm sun to dry, listen to the steady roar of the waterfall as the water rolls over the rocks around you. Notice how it has smoothed the rocks, a process that takes many, many years. Notice how perfect the waterfall is, how beautiful the surroundings are, how your cares are washing away. With each breath, take in the serenity of your surroundings and let yourself release all that has troubled you, all that you find unacceptable. Trust that your Higher Power is making everything as perfect as your surroundings. Know that you do not need to struggle with anything anymore. Everything is now acceptable in your Higher Power's eyes. Embrace this truth in grateful humility.

Chapter 6

Breaking Free

STEP EIGHT: Made a list of all persons we had harmed, and became willing to make amends to them all.

Most of our troubles in life have to do with relationships. We are often distressed when we are at odds with other people. Steps Eight and Nine give us the means to clear up the problem areas in our relationships. They do this in a very direct manner—by asking us to identify and to make amends to those people we have harmed.

"But I'm not the one to blame," we caregivers are inclined to protest. "I'm the one with the added burdens. I'm the one who gets walked on. Other people should be making amends to *me!*" Our denial is quickly evident in these statements. Step Eight asks us to list people we have harmed, but instead we often turn that around and start listing the people who have harmed us. It's much easier to see the faults of others, to feel sorry for ourselves, to indulge in self-righteousness.

We may indeed have suffered some injuries from others. But focusing on their wrongs, as a way to excuse our own, will only keep us swimming in self-pity and discontent. After all, we can't control the behavior of others. But we are responsible for our own. So, for Step Eight, we need to keep the focus on ourselves and what we have done to make or keep our relationships unsatisfactory.

This calls for another honest and deep moral search. In Steps Four and Five, we courageously uncovered and admitted our shortcomings. Now, our task is to face the specific consequences of our actions and set things right. We need to be painstaking in recalling patterns and incidents that damaged our relationships. We also need to write down the names of those we hurt. Why write them? It is a way to make this Step very concrete. It helps us to be honest and to grasp fully the implications of what we have done. We see not only our wrongs, but the names of the individual people affected by them. We see exactly what our actions have done to others, as well as what these actions have cost us. Writing the names down also keeps us from the denial that often comes up; we can so easily "forget" the names of people who may be hard to make amends to.

Why It's Necessary

But couldn't we just let bygones be bygones? Do we have to bring up the past? That's a little like asking if we can walk away from a car accident we have caused without taking care of the damages. Wanting to just forget about the harmful things we have done comes from two attitudes—pride and fear. We want others to think well of us, and we want to think well of ourselves. And we think that we can only have this respect if we are seen by others or by ourselves as perfect. Well, the truth is that we aren't perfect, and we don't have to be perfect to earn genuine respect. But we do have to be honest. If we behave as if we have done nothing wrong when the people around us are stinging from our actions, we are letting our prideful ego take center stage. We are not letting people know who we really are. And how can anyone love and respect us if they don't know us?

The goal of Steps Eight and Nine, however, is not to gain love and respect from others, although that may be one outcome. Rather, it is to identify and make amends to those we have harmed. That may indeed be a setback for our pride, at least initially. It can be hard on our ego to think about going to someone and acknowledging our wrongdoings. Not only is our pride threatened, but we may become fearful about other consequences. What if the person becomes angry? What if we are laughed at? What if the person won't talk to us? We can come up with a long list of worries that may deter us from our amends process.

But we do not have to fret about what might happen—that's living in the future. Instead, we can bring ourselves back to the present and remember that we are asked in Step Eight only to make the list of people we have harmed, and to be willing to make amends. We concern ourselves with just these tasks and trust that Step Nine will take care of itself. As we begin our list, we can ask our Higher Power for guidance in completing it.

Making the List

Referring to our inventory, we list everyone we have harmed—relatives, friends, acquaintances, employers and other work associates, people who provide services for us, and so on. Whether or not our harmful actions toward them were deliberate, we include their names on the list. We even include those who may not have been aware of the damage we caused. Thoroughness and honesty are important here, just as they were in doing our Fourth Step inventory.

Peace with Ourselves

Our own name deserves a special place on the list because we often hurt ourselves. Through such shortcomings as isolation, bitterness, manipulation, or blaming, we have deprived ourselves of the benefits of close, caring relationships with others. If we have been fearful, we may have numbed a part of ourselves that is spontaneous and daring. If we have been taking on more than our share of responsibility, we may have worn ourselves out. Many of us have bogged ourselves down in guilt and shame. When we criticize ourselves too much, we damage our self-esteem. We have sometimes allowed others to make unreasonable demands on us and treat us poorly. We may fail to get enough rest, nourishment, privacy, and emotional support. We may have let discouragement, even depression, stop us from enjoying life.

Before we can expect to set right our relations with others, we would do well to acknowledge and forgive what we have done to ourselves. If we are at peace with ourselves, we bring more integrity to the process of making peace with others and asking for their forgiveness.

To begin finding peace with ourselves requires complete honesty, neither exaggerating our wrongdoings nor underplaying them as we make our list. We acknowledge fully our part in what occurred, but we do not take on unwarranted responsibility. We avoid extremes. We accept the guilt where it is ours, without becoming totally demoralized by it. We do not wallow in the guilt, nor condemn ourselves. We simply prepare to acknowledge the damage we caused, and become willing to make amends and the necessary changes required to ensure it doesn't happen anymore.

Making amends is more than making an apology. The goal is to change our thoughts and behaviors. This is not easy, and it is not to be taken lightly. In some cases, it involves uprooting lifelong ways of behaving. In Step Seven, we have already asked for help from our Higher Power to make these changes. Now we get the opportunity to direct these changes toward specific relationships.

Honesty

Some of us can readily identify the people we have harmed. We know who has taken the brunt of our angry outbursts. We see clearly where we have hurt others through being critical or refusing their help or failing to follow through on our promises to them. We know whom we have cheated, lied to, or rejected. In looking at our relationships with the people we care for, we remember clearly the times we have reacted poorly—perhaps with disgust or embarrassment—to some of their actions. We know the times we have expected too much of them or insisted on doing for them what they could and preferred to do for themselves.

For those of us that still doubt we have any amends to make to anyone but ourselves, making our list will demand a new level of honesty. The harm that we do may be very subtle. We can begin by checking to see if we have become so absorbed in our own needs—perhaps perpetually feeling self-pity—that we are not able to see the genuine needs of others. Do we feel certain we know what's best for others when the truth is that they are capable of making their own choices? If we do, no doubt we communicate that in subtle, or maybe not so subtle, ways. Have we used our fears, our laziness, our busyness as excuses for shunning our responsibilities? Have we failed to be honest with others because they might get too angry or because we have decided they are too old or sick? Have we let the fear of our own emotions keep us from allowing others to express theirs? Have we tried to make others feel guilty for not doing enough? Have we tried to control others?

We must again remind ourselves that we are not searching our soul in order to punish ourselves. Rather, our intention is to clear away anything from our past and present that doesn't serve us well. We want to make way for new, positive thoughts and actions.

Becoming Willing to Change

Once our list of people we have harmed is made, the second half of this Step asks us to become willing to make amends to them all. We need to consider, as we did in Step Six, what it means to *become willing*. In some cases, becoming willing may be the hardest thing we ever have to do in our Twelve Step program. We may feel some people have hurt us so badly or are so nasty that we could never make amends to them. We are angry with them and we intend to stay angry. Whatever we've done to them, we may feel they deserved it.

Making amends to these people won't come easily for many of us. It may take awhile before we free ourselves from the self-will that keeps us holding on to our anger. Certainly, we can't become entirely willing to make these amends by ourselves. We need to turn once again to our Higher Power and ask for the willingness. We may not be willing right away, but as we make our other amends and continue to Let Go and Let God, we may find that eventually we can make those amends and be free of our inner turmoil. Along the way, we can learn to be patient with ourselves, even forgiving the weaknesses we exhibit in carrying out this Step.

Forgiveness is a big part of doing Step Eight. Along with forgiving ourselves and asking forgiveness of others, we need to *offer* forgiveness. Perhaps it is only in giving forgiveness that we can be ready to receive it. Knowing that our own short-comings can be so insidious and so hard to give up, we can be more understanding of others' shortcomings. By forgiving, we give up the grudge we may be holding over others. We see ourselves as neither better nor worse than they are. We are equals. In fact, this may give us greater peace of mind. We no longer have to diminish ourselves by comparing ourselves to someone we think is better. We can love ourselves and others as we are. At the same time, we can be open to further growth and change. We are like the acorn that is planted and grows into a unique and beautiful oak tree, even if some of the branches get bent by a strong wind or the trunk gets stunted by a drought.

Even though Step Eight appears to be a rather passive Step (merely writing a list and becoming willing), it really requires growth to deepen our understanding and appreciation of what it means to be human. This Step is also necessary for us to become ready for Step Nine.

EXERCISE: MAKING YOUR LIST

Make out a list of people you have harmed. Ask your Higher Power for guidance to make sure your list is complete. Consider each name on the list and ask yourself if you are ready to change your way of dealing with this person. This may mean developing a closer, more caring relationship with some people. With others, you may decide that you need to separate yourself from them, at least for a time. Ask your Higher Power for the wisdom and courage to make the necessary changes.

EXERCISE: BECOMING WILLING

Some names on your list may upset you. You may feel you can't forgive them, you may be afraid of their reaction to an amend, or you may not be ready to give up your familiar way of doing things. For each of these people, try the following activities to help you develop the willingness asked for in Step Eight:

- Write out your upsetting feelings about each person on paper. Keep writing, in detail, until you have nothing more to say. Then take some time to release these feelings to your Higher Power. To make this experience as meaningful as possible, you can tear the paper into little pieces and throw them away. Another way to symbolically release your feelings is to place the paper in a bowl and burn it in a special ceremony with one or more friends as witnesses.

- Close your eyes and imagine holding a large, beautiful golden globe of healing light in your hands. Allow the globe to grow larger and larger until you can step inside it. Picture the person who upsets you inside the globe with you. Let the light fill you with love and compassion. See the other person through the eyes of love. Now picture yourself finding a peaceful resolution regarding your upsetting feelings toward this person. Take as much time as you need. Picture yourself making peace with this person. Or, if you are guided by your Higher Power to separate from this person, imagine yourself lovingly releasing this person from your life. Take in the love and forgiveness represented by the globe of light. Feel its warmth. Keep that warmth and love in your heart as you leave the globe, and then open your eyes.

Whether you use a quiet prayer, a dramatic symbol, or a mental image, take this opportunity to release yourself from the bonds that keep you tied to the past or fearful of the future.

STEP NINE: Made direct amends to such people wherever possible, except when to do so would injure them or others.

Step Nine opens the door to a new life for many of us. It gives us the opportunity to clear everything from our past so that we can move ahead freely.

Our work in the previous Steps has prepared us for this action Step. We are now clear about our wrongdoings. With our Higher Power in charge of removing our shortcomings, we can live freely now; we can stop punishing others when they don't do things our way; and we can accept the conditions we can't change. And we now know what amends need to be made to those we've hurt in the past, and we have become willing to make those amends.

Facing Step Nine requires courage and humility. It's easy to become too busy or too frightened or to decide something else is more important than doing this Step. But we can't allow ourselves to make any excuses. It's time to begin.

How to Make Amends

We need to make plans to contact each person, one at a time. We can begin anywhere we wish on our list. Some people like to get the most difficult amends over with right away; others prefer to save them until last. Some people approach the friends or relatives they feel closest to first. For others, those amends are the hardest to handle, and they prefer to start with those people they're not as emotionally close to. There is no right order for making amends. Our Higher Power is our reliable guide.

Making the amends in person is always preferable. It is a good idea to set aside a special time with each person on our list just for this purpose. We approach each person with humility and speak honestly and candidly. We acknowledge what we have done, explain our plans to take care of any damages, and explain how we will alter our behavior. If we want forgiveness, we need to ask for it.

The following guidelines can help when meeting with each person on our list:

- We speak only of *our* actions and take full responsibility for them. We do not try to justify them or disguise them.
- We never call attention to the other person's failings, nor do we expect him or her to reciprocate with amends. We remember that our purpose is to make amends for our own wrongdoings.
- We are clear and direct in our message.
- We accept forgiveness, but we do not demand it. We try to make peace to the extent the person is willing, but we

don't try to force them into a relationship with us.

- We are grateful if the person is understanding and shows appreciation, but we try not to become disturbed by other reactions.
- Whatever the other person's reaction, we keep our purpose in mind and avoid retaliating or getting defensive.

Not every person we have harmed can be contacted in person. Some amends are made by telephone or letter, using the same guidelines. We need to do everything we can to be forthright with each person and to accept the consequences of their response.

Those We Cannot Contact

We cannot make direct amends to some people because we may not know how to find them, or it may not be safe for us to contact them. We must be as vigilant and honest as we can, however, to make sure we are not avoiding anyone on our list simply because the amends may be difficult. We try to find people who have moved away. We do our best to determine whether contacting the person can be done safely. If, for example, someone might physically harm us or is unapproachable because of their alcoholic behavior, we have to be cautious.

For those people on our list who are dead or who we cannot contact, we can write a letter, even if it cannot be mailed. Or the amends can be done with someone who represents the person, such as a member of the person's family or perhaps a spiritual director or friend. These approaches are also helpful if the person we are making amends to is mentally incapable of understanding what we say—a person with Alzheimer's disease, for example.

Rita Makes Amends

Rita made amends to her deceased father during a time

of meditation and prayer. "I feel that I was heard. I feel forgiven." She also wanted to make amends to her mother, whom she resented so much for not expressing love to her. Through Step Nine, Rita wanted to release herself from the self-destructive resentments she had carried within her for so long. One day, as she went through her mother's personal belongings, she was taken by surprise. There Rita found the many special cards and letters she had sent her mother from years past. Rita choked up. "I didn't know they mattered to her." She began to cry. "I see my mother differently now. I think now that she loved me even though she couldn't express it."

Rita also wanted to release the embarrassment and guilt she often felt over her mother's behavior in the nursing home. "I went in to see her one day and she had knocked down everything in another person's room. It just made me sick." Rita quickly found the person and blurted out, "I'm so sorry! I feel just terrible. You know my mom didn't mean it. She doesn't realize what she's doing." Later, Rita realized that she took on the guilt and shame for what her mother did and made excuses for her. As Rita progresses in her Twelve Step program, the guilt and shame she feels are diminishing. "I remind myself that I'm not responsible for her behavior," she says.

Because of her mother's present inability to communicate rationally, Rita could not make amends to her mother in words. But she is making changes in the way she treats her mother. "I have tried to make amends by supporting her now, by touching and hugging her. I gently rub her legs or hold her hands when she gets jumpy."

Rita is also making amends to herself. Through using the Twelve Steps to examine her life, Rita discovered she has gotten into numerous friendships with people who act like her mother used to—as she says, "people who put me down in subtle ways." She has one friend who is very much like her mother. "I was always trying to get approval from her. But I have worked things out with her now. I no longer need her approval. She no longer judges or advises me."

Joining Overeaters Anonymous helped Rita lose the weight she gained when her mother still stayed with her. But she remembers that after she lost the weight and bought a new suit, "I felt so good, but my mother never even noticed. That hurt so bad. But I found out later that she did mention it to someone else."

Rita still yearns for the love she never felt from her mother. But she also recognizes how she held back her own love as well. "I regret now that I didn't let her know I loved her, and that I didn't try harder to see if I could open the door to her feelings a little more. Now I can only imagine that door being open, that she loves me. And for my own peace of mind, I have to do that now."

Making Amends to Ourselves

Making amends to ourselves is extremely important for caregivers. We begin by forgiving ourselves for what we have done to others, as well as to ourselves. We need to make changes so that we can treat ourselves with respect. One way to do this is to set boundaries. This means deciding what we can and will do, and then doing only that. We also need to stop doing for others what they can do for themselves. We can't let the actions of others dominate our life. We have to make sure our basic needs are met—getting enough rest, eating healthy, having companionship or love. We need to ask for help. Whenever the burdens of caregiving feel like they are too much for us, they probably are.

Making amends to ourselves can mean taking decisive action when that is what's needed. For example, Lisa and her sisters were worried when their eighty-seven-year-old mother, despite her developing health problems, protested the idea of leaving her home and living in a semi-independent residence for the frail elderly. Yet, she called her daughters several times a day because she was so lonely. They worried constantly that she might have a medical emergency at home with no one there to help. They soon decided to give up their constant worry and feeling sorry for her and insisted she make the move. She gave in reluctantly, and now she and her daughters are all pleased with the arrangement. Lisa's mother greatly enjoys the company of the other people in the residence and eagerly joins in organizing activities there. Now she is so busy, her daughters jokingly complain that they have a hard time finding her available when they call.

Amends to ourselves can be a matter of setting priorities and eliminating activities that interfere with them, as Marlene has done. Marlene, who is in her seventies and whose husband has Parkinson's disease, has decided to change her ways. "I'm a perfectionist. I'm learning not to be because it's a pain in the neck." She is concerned about her failing heart and wants to stay as healthy as possible. Because of this, she has modified some of her activities. "I have always loved to give dinner parties. I still have them, but I don't go all out like I used to. I make some of the food the night before, and instead of a fancy dessert, I serve ice cream. I have a lot of things to live for."

Still, Marlene admitted that she is set in her ways. "I'm very strong-minded, stubborn. That's a character defect. It makes more sense to be easygoing. I have to ask forgiveness." She also struggles with Step Nine when it comes to forgiving others. "I know I can't hold grudges, but I do sometimes. Some people have hurt me so badly, I can't forgive them. I don't feel it's possible. I can't change them, so I just detach and stay away from them."

Detachment

Detaching is another way to make amends to ourselves.

Detachment is a tool for caregivers who want to recover their sanity around the people whose behavior they find disturbing. Whether or not we physically separate from someone, we can detach ourselves mentally and emotionally from their behavior. The trick is to become observers and refuse to be drawn in by their behavior or to feel responsible for it. We can stay centered within ourselves. We may never be able to feel complete love for them, but at least we can stop judging or blaming them. We concern ourselves only with taking care of our own business and being responsible for our own actions.

> *Diane:* I gave Frances so much power. I wanted her to think of me as being the very best. We did so many things for her. We even had a family "Frances night" once a week where we served her favorite dish, and the kids would entertain her after dinner. But Frances would make cutting remarks, and she would write to her friends about how mistreated she was. When she didn't want to hear something, she would turn off her hearing aid. Our kids would sometimes get mad at me for putting up with her. We'd have family arguments about it. I would tell them, "Don't feel that way." I would try to smooth everything over. Then I would walk out, blaming everybody else for the way they were treating her.
>
> Then, when Frances went to a nursing home, I at first felt I had to go there every day to make sure everything was taken care of. She was always after me to bring her things, and she complained about being there. She wanted my pity. But as I gained self-respect, I detached from her demanding and manipulative ways. I told Frances, "I will come when I can, but not every day." The reality is that she was being well taken care of there, and I wanted to visit her when I enjoyed being there. The same is true with

my mother. Then, when I go, it's not out of guilt or duty, but out of fondness.

Step Nine is about change, and as shown, many changes take thoughtful soul-searching, courage, and respect for others as well as ourselves. Amends are not trivial apologies to be quickly gotten through. They are an ongoing part of our daily Twelve Step living, with practical applications.

Learning new attitudes and behaviors takes time and usually some experimentation. Step Nine helps us get off to a good start when we state our intentions directly to others. Asking for the support of others to carry out these intentions is also a good idea.

The Benefits of Making Amends

As we make our amends, we often enjoy many benefits. We become free of guilt and resentment that have bogged us down. We grow in love, self-respect, courage, and confidence. We become more at ease with ourselves and our circumstances. We become more authentic in our relations with the people we care for, and with the other people in our life.

For example, Flora speaks of how angry she sometimes gets with the burden of caring for both her frail mother and her neighbor with AIDS. "I wonder, *Where is the person who can take care of me?* I get resentful of my kids not doing more for me. Sometimes I feel like a dog under the table waiting for somebody to spill some crumbs. But I don't tell my kids what my needs are. Instead, my anger and frustration escalate, and I find myself slamming doors. When I acknowledge and articulate my needs, some kind of healing takes place; a burden is lifted."

The second part of Step Nine asks us to be prudent in carrying out our amends. We need to make every effort not to cause further harm when we acknowledge our past wrongdoings. If some of our actions involved others who might be implicated, we must be careful. Will their reputation be harmed by our revelation? Can the person to whom we make amends be trusted with information revealed about others? We cannot hesitate to make amends, however, simply because a person might be upset by something we say.

We can set aside our fears when we turn over to our Higher Power the outcome of our making amends. We do our part as honestly and respectfully as possible—that is all Step Nine asks. We can then enjoy relief from past burdens. We are free to live in the present, One Day at a Time.

EXERCISE: PRACTICING AMENDS

Practice can make the amends process go much more smoothly. Practice in front of a mirror, or ask a trusted friend or a professional counselor to allow you to practice making the amends that frighten you. Ask the stand-in to act just as you suspect the actual person will behave. As you role-play your amends, you will get a sense of what detachment means, because you will probably not get as upset by the stand-in's behavior as you might with the recipient of your amend. This will help you become more at ease. You can then maintain this attitude during the actual meeting. Don't worry if you can't make amends perfectly in every situation. Simply turn each meeting over to your Higher Power and do the best you can.

EXERCISE: ACCEPTING SLIPUPS

Find a piece of paper that has been rolled up or bent. Try to straighten it. You will notice it does not regain its original form easily. In the same way, the amends or changes you want to make will take repeated attempts in most cases. You may even find yourself slipping back into old habits, just as the piece of paper tends to roll up again. This is normal. Be patient with yourself. Use these slipups as a reminder to be patient and compassionate with others around you—who may be also doing their best. Continue your Twelve Step work daily, and you will make the necessary changes over time.

Chapter 7

Finding Strength Day by Day

STEP TEN: Continued to take personal inventory and when
we were wrong promptly admitted it.

How easy it would be to feel we are done with the program
after Step Nine. After all, we have acknowledged our depend-
ence on and surrendered our life to God. We have surveyed
our character defects, asked God to remove them, and made
amends to those people whom we have harmed. We have
cleared up our past and are ready for a fresh start. Gradually,
we have found more peace of mind. With all this, we could
be satisfied.

But the Twelve Steps constitute a lifelong process of spiritual growth for caregivers. And just as the care of our loved
one calls for our daily attention, so does our spiritual growth.
The remaining three Steps help us to foster this growth on a
daily basis. Step Ten invites us to pay attention to our
thoughts and actions, to regularly clean up any wrongdoing,
and to focus on the new behaviors we want to acquire. Step
Eleven puts us in daily contact with our source of power. Step
Twelve encourages us to draw on the program principles
throughout each day and to share our experience with others.

We may have released the emotional pain of yesterday, but the temptation to slip into our old ways of doing things could trip us up if we are not vigilant. New challenges also come along as the circumstances in our life change. In addition, even though we were thorough in our Step work until now, our insight and wisdom can continue to expand. As we practice the program daily, we see additional habits to change or fine-tune.

Daily Inventory

Step Ten gives us a daily structure for maintaining our program. It is a way to catch and re-direct ourselves if we should start to detour from our spiritual path. In the past, often we have slipped into long periods of feeling guilty, depressed, or angry over something that happened. Once we started obsessing about some occurrence, we couldn't seem to stop. Now, with a daily inventory, we notice quickly when we start a downward slide. We can respond promptly by using the Steps. We recognize our powerlessness and insanity in day-to-day situations, and we turn our worries as well as our mistakes over to our Higher Power at once. If amends are necessary, we make them without delay.

To do this, we form a new habit of daily self-examination. Many people do their daily inventory at the end of the day. A good time is when we brush our teeth or as we climb into bed. In the same way that we decide whether to toss the clothes we were wearing into the laundry, hang them up, wash them out, or leave them out till morning, we can briefly review the behavior we "wore" during the day. Did we get caught up in jealousy, resentment, controlling, self-condemnation? Did we use our caregiving responsibilities as an excuse for self-pity or anger? Did we judge others, fail to take care of ourselves, allow ourselves to be manipulated, gossip, or lie? Some people find it helpful to keep by their bed or on their mirror a daily checklist of the habitual behaviors they want to change, based on their Fourth Step inventory.

Honesty and forgiveness keep us on track as we review the day. We acknowledge what happened, and we forgive ourselves and others for any harm done. Then we make plans for any necessary amends. The progress we make daily in our spiritual path also deserves our attention. We express appreciation for our progress, knowing that progress, not perfection, is our goal. After turning everything over to our Higher Power, a restful night without worry or guilt is our reward.

> *The Larsens: In our household, the two of us conduct our inventories together each morning in prayer and preparation for the day. We see this time as an opportunity for daily renewal. We each take a few moments to acknowledge our impatience or irritability or other shortcomings. We also make commitments to each other about changes we wish to make.*
>
> *The importance of this daily inventory and renewal came home to us so strongly when Frances died. Suddenly all the things we got so irritated about didn't seem so important. Her death put us more in touch with our own mortality too. We realize we have only today, and that each day should be celebrated.*

A daily journal is another way many caregivers keep track of their progress. By writing about our daily activities and concerns, we sometimes see them more clearly. We may also act more quickly to clear them up. Over time, some patterns may become evident. For example, we may notice that we repeatedly write about our resentment over one person's behavior, giving us a clue that a more in-depth inventory may be needed to get to the bottom of the problems in that relationship.

Long-Term Inventory

Once or twice a year, taking a long-term inventory to examine our patterns is a good idea. Some people take a day or two away at a retreat or in a quiet setting to review their spiritual progress. Others talk things over with a friend or spiritual director. It may mean engaging a substitute caregiver for a time, but the serenity offered by the Twelve Steps is so valuable, we become willing to do whatever is necessary to keep and deepen it.

This long-term inventory presents a new opportunity to get perspective on behaviors that have become so routine that we have not rooted them out during our daily inventory. They are too deeply planted in us. We need to spend time facing them honestly and examining in-depth what keeps us stuck in self-destructive ways. We ask for greater clarity, open ourselves to God's working within us, and consider any amends we must make. We take advantage of the support God offers in the process of removing these defects. In addition to the daily inventory and long-term inventory, we can spot-check our behavior throughout each day. We take note when we feel disturbed about something and are hanging on to that feeling. Normally, a persistent disturbance to our peace of mind means that our self-will is trying to take over the direction of our life. We use this opportunity to realign ourselves with God's will.

Flora's Method of Coping

Flora, for example, finds that resentment and self-pity come creeping into her consciousness all too easily when she spends large amounts of time taking care of both her mother and the dying man in the neighboring apartment. Her self-will promotes grandiosity, helping her believe, on the one hand, that she is indispensable, and on the other hand, that others should automatically know she needs help and come to her rescue. During frequent prayerful moments throughout the day (her form of spot-check inventory), Flora reminds herself that her Higher Power is in charge. Resuming her trust and serenity, she does what she can, asks for the help she needs, and leaves the rest in her Higher Power's hands.

HALT

A helpful tool for keeping us on track is HALT, an acronym that reminds us to beware of becoming too Hungry, Angry, Lonely, or Tired. A spot-check should quickly alert us if one of these triggers for trouble is present. We can then do whatever we need to do to take care of ourselves so that none of our destructive habits is set off.

Gentleness

Sometimes frightening thoughts that make us feel ashamed come up in our inventories. We may try to shut them off because we think they are bad. Fortunately, this practice of denying or feeling ashamed of such thoughts cannot survive long if we are working our program. As our honesty grows, we become willing to express those thoughts and the accompanying feelings of shame to our Higher Power and to someone who is understanding and trustworthy.

For example, caregivers sometimes wish the person who is suffering would die. This may seem like an awful thought, but it's the truth. And we can easily sink into intense guilt for reacting that way. We condemn ourselves for being selfish or vicious. But we do not need to label ourselves or our reactions as bad. Caring for someone suffering with a chronic condition can be very painful and draining— physically, emotionally, and mentally. It is normal to want some final relief for the affected person and for ourselves.

An important ingredient in all our inventories is gentleness.

As the burdens become extremely heavy for us and we feel like giving up, we will benefit more from compassion and gentleness than from self-condemnation. For a time, perhaps all we can do is to express our frustration with the situation and our wish that it were over. Within ourselves, we can seek reassurance that God's will is guiding the universe perfectly, and we can seek serenity in surrender. If that does not come easily, we try to be patient with ourselves. We know that our thoughts and feelings, even the harsh ones, are part of God's plan, and that we are loved and cared for, no matter what.

Sharing Our Journey

Sharing our difficulties with an understanding friend or professional often helps. One day, Odella got a call from a woman whose son, suffering from cancer, had been given no further hope by his physicians. Odella's friend needed somebody to talk to, and since Odella had a daughter with leukemia, the woman felt she might understand. The woman revealed to Odella that she was hoping her son would die quickly. Yet, she was consumed with guilt about this thought.

Odella remembers how they talked and cried together for a long time. "We both decided that wishing your child would die rather than have him go on suffering was a very normal reaction. The best thing we could do was to talk about it, to offer each other a little bit of love and support, even though we didn't have any answers."

Our inventories help us get used to honesty, and that honesty naturally flows over into our relations with others. Honesty was a great help to Odella and her family in getting through the fifteen years of her daughter's illness. "Somewhere along the line, I came to the realization that if I simply stated how I was feeling and why I was feeling that way, and did that openly and honestly, that made it easier for everybody. If we did something wrong, instead of feeling bad, we would say, 'I yelled, and I'm really sorry; I was just so worried.' We found that if we were honest and told each other, it became much easier to understand and to forgive each other. Sometimes we would have shouting matches where everybody was talking at once, but we would end up with everybody laughing and saying, 'Now, I understand.'"

Ongoing honesty gives us freedom. We don't have to hide things from others or ourselves. We become more at ease with ourselves and our world. We are able to give and receive love freely because we understand that each of us is suffering in some way and doing the best we can with our life. There can be great joy in that discovery. The burden of having to be so careful and so perfect is lifted. Yet, we are free to change and grow when that is helpful. Step Ten helps us deepen our honesty and decrease our resistance to growth.

EXERCISE: DAILY INVENTORY

Examine your daily routine and select a time to regularly do a daily inventory. A reminder might be to place an inventory checklist on your desk or a bedside table—somewhere that you'll see it at that particular time of day. Write out the procedure you will use for your inventory. It may be as simple as

- Pray for honesty.
- Review my checklist.
- Acknowledge my wrongdoings.
- Forgive.
- Plan amends.
- Re-commit.
- Thank God.

EXERCISE: SPOT-CHECK INVENTORY

Identify checkpoints during the day (such as right before lunch or on the way home from work) when you can do regular spot-checks. Ask yourself: In the past few hours, have I been caught up in worry, guilt, anger, or other troubling emotions? Have I been expecting too much of myself? Have I tried to control others? Have my attitudes and actions made me feel separate from my Higher Power? From others? From myself?

EXERCISE: LONG-TERM INVENTORY

Begin making plans now for a long-term inventory. Decide what arrangements you need to make. Set this as a priority. Give it to yourself as a gift. Acknowledge any resistance you feel, and ask your Higher Power to melt away that resistance.

EXERCISE: SUPPORT SYSTEM

Identify people who will listen to you and can help you with honesty, compassion, and commitment to your growth. If they can also help you laugh at your mistakes, all the better.

> STEP ELEVEN: Sought through prayer and meditation to improve our conscious contact with God *as we understood God,* praying only for knowledge of God's will and the power to carry that out.

The Twelve Steps represent a spiritual program. In the first three Steps, recognizing our powerlessness and our insane thinking, we caregivers gave ourselves over to God or some other form of Higher Power. In Step Five, we admitted our wrongs to God. In Step Seven, we turned to God again, asking for freedom from our shortcomings. By now, we may be seeing the miracles God has worked in our life. We're feeling less frantic and less burdened. Our relationships are more satisfying. Because we take better care of ourselves, we have more to give, and we give more freely. We have so much already to be grateful to God for.

Naturally, we want to keep developing this spirituality.

Step Eleven gives us a way to do this on a daily basis—prayer and meditation. Using these gifts deepens our conscious contact with God. They are the daily bread that nourishes our spirituality.

Resistance

Two types of people may be tempted to ignore this Step: Those of us who already pray routinely think we don't need it; those of us who want nothing to do with prayer or even God, for that matter, eye this Step with disdain, or at least suspicion. In the second case, we may have developed our feelings as a result of negative experiences early in our life. In both cases, our opinions may be strong. Our views are set. As far as we're concerned, this Step is irrelevant and impractical.

What makes us so sure? Haven't we previously been sure about a lot of things that we now judge as more or less insane choices? Haven't we yet seen enough evidence that insisting on our own ego's choices brings deep troubles? Can we honestly say we have embraced Step Three if we are still holding out, thinking we know what's best for us?

Those of us who resist Step Eleven for a time and finally see the wisdom of giving it a fresh ear hear a fresh melody. If we already pray routinely, we develop some new perspectives on our prayer life. We see that some of our prayers have become, in fact, quite routine. In some cases, we find we are still reciting by rote our childhood prayers though they retain little meaning for us. Others of us realize that we have turned prayer into a list of "give me" requests, treating God pretty much like a delivery service. We think we know what is best for ourselves and others; we measure our success and our worthiness by how well God delivers on our requests. Yet, as caregivers, we have often been disappointed in the results of this kind of prayer.

Still others of us who have been faithful with our prayers

carry a view of God as a punitive judge, always watching for us to trip up. We have prayed out of fear all our life.

A great many of us, despite our best intentions of praying and meditating, simply don't take the time.

For those of us who initially rejected the notion of God or prayer, Step Eleven becomes an opportunity to reconsider this from our new perspective. We see others, who have years of experience with the Twelve Steps, finding consolation and hope in their prayer life. We see our own life changing dramatically through our willingness to surrender to the wisdom of the previous Steps. If the other Steps have worked so well, might this one too be worth exploring in more depth?

Deepening Our Spirituality

Once we get beyond our hesitations and become willing to be seekers, as Step Eleven suggests, rather than know-it-alls, we are astounded at what happens. Our openness to Step Eleven takes us into a deeper spirituality. We come into close contact with a God of unconditional love and compassion. Knowing God's will and living by it become our only goals. Through daily conscious contact with our Higher Power, we now find our every action guided. Our way becomes clearer. We now have confidence, knowing that we are constantly supported and loved. We are relieved that we don't have to depend on our own weak will to get us through emotional disturbances. We align ourselves more and more with God's will and find peace of mind therein.

Rita has changed how she sees God's will. "God's will isn't 'You have to.' When I think of God's will, I think of peace, happiness, joy. It's what I do for myself as well as others."

Caregivers Find Help in Prayer and Meditation

Marvin: I have the feeling of living in the presence of God much of the time. In my business, I don't think I would survive without contact with God. I have virtually no control over how people are going to respond. I end up praying a lot, although not necessarily in words. It gives me a degree of serenity and I can keep functioning and not become dispirited.

Jean hasn't yet figured out how to handle the daily complaint calls from her ailing mother, but she finds strength each day in God. "I spend a lot of time on my prayer bones," she says. "I've even been angry at God, but God has big shoulders. He can take it."

People in Twelve Step programs practice many forms of prayer and meditation. Each individual finds a unique path to God. What is important is not the form, but the sincerity of the person.

Defining Prayer

Prayer is defined as the lifting of our heart and mind to our Higher Power. We simply turn the attention of our heart and mind toward God. We express the awe and gratitude we experience for all the daily miracles of our life—the plants and trees that unfold from tiny seeds, the courage and love we see in others and ourselves, our every breath—and the many other wonders we can see in each day when we pause to reflect.

As we become aware that God's will for us governs and guides all that is, we ask only "for knowledge of God's will for us and the power to carry that out." Those are the exact words of Step Eleven. Yet, caught up in our own self-will, a lot of us would perhaps rather gloss over that. We *still* think we know what's best for us, and we want to bend God's ear to hear our give-me list. That's all right. God is perfectly willing to listen to our needs and wants. But to help us with our ongoing process of surrender, it's a good idea to add "if it be Your will" at the end of those requests. Otherwise, we might think it is our prayers or our actions that merit a reward or rejection. That's just another way of trying to hang on to some of the control, instead of surrendering to our Higher Power.

However we bring ourselves to prayer, we are welcomed by God's unconditional love. Our prayer is not an attempt to please God. Rather, we try to tune in to God's wavelength, to the universal love that is ours if we choose to accept it. That's where meditation comes in.

Defining Meditation

Meditation is a time of being receptive, of listening. We have opened ourselves up to know God's will. Now we listen for what God offers us. We try to do this at a quiet time, away from distractions. We relax and open our heart and mind. We don't expect to hear a voice giving us specific directions in words, although some people report such occurrences. More likely, we get frequent insights about things happening in our life, a sense of knowing what is right for us.

This sense of inner knowing will stay with us throughout the day, guiding our every action. At first, this may be hard for us to recognize, but little by little, we start to see how guidance comes to us during our day in ways we hadn't noticed before. We feel a sense of calm in an explosive situation. We see new options available where, before, only one outcome had been apparent. We laugh instead of panic.

Over time, we become confident that God's will is being expressed in each event in our life. When that is not immediately evident, a brief time of meditation may enlighten us. We may see a child playing as a reminder to release our worries and center ourselves in the here and now. Focusing our attention on a tiny tree bud may offer a sign of hope. We use someone's annoying behavior as a reminder that we have amends of our own to make. Paying attention to a deep sadness within us, we surrender to the grief rather than take a compulsive drink or bite.

Practical Spirituality
   It's a very practical matter really.

Diane: When Frances was dying, our life was full with work and school and a lot of things happening in our family. It was a very emotional time. Besides dealing with the day-to-day uncertainties of Frances's condition, we were preparing to host a baby shower for our daughter and expecting the birth of a grandchild very soon. And, always, there was the concern for how my mother was doing. One day, I remember going into the basement for something. But what grabbed my attention at the bottom of the stairs were the piles of Frances's discarded clothes stacked there. My mind just went into a frenzy. Not one more thing to take care of! It took a few moments, but I said a quick prayer, took a deep breath, and remembered One Day at a Time. That was enough to calm me down. Wouldn't you know when I came back upstairs, the phone rang! It was a charitable organization asking for clothes donations and they were willing to pick them up. Sometimes God's will shows up in neon lights!

   In the morning, the time the two of us spend together includes readings, prayer and meditation, as well as our inventories and commitment to change. We pray for ourselves and for many people individually, making specific requests. We always keep in mind, "Not my will, but thine, be done." Frequent moments of prayer and meditation throughout the day reinforce the morning devotion.

Marvin: Any time I am facing a decision, I ask myself, "Is this expressing love?" If it is, then I go ahead with it.

For caregivers, daily contact with our Higher Power is important because it keeps us confident that we are on the right track. Some of us may make this contact through a time of quiet contemplation on a word, an object, an idea, or, as we have described, a time of listening to the wisdom that comes from deep within. Some of us pray on the way to and from work. Others ask for guidance at bedtime. We may take advantage of the many minutes or even hours we spend in tiresome waiting—in doctor's waiting rooms, for example—to seek the serenity of connecting with our Higher Power.

Meditation Books Help Marlene

Marlene uses the time when her husband takes a bath to sit by the window with a cup of coffee and think of pleasant things. Sometimes she reads from meditation books. Explaining her meditation process, Marlene quotes Abraham Lincoln's famous line, "Most folks are about as happy as they make up their minds to be." She adds, "I think of that a lot. I try to adjust to what is. I try to like what I have, if I can't change it." Her connection with her Higher Power is based on her religious beliefs. "I feel like God is within me. I see a picture of God with me. I feel like God's guiding me." The meditation books help relieve her guilt and worry, she says. "I seem to be able to not dwell on problems."

Flora's Shining Light

When Flora meditates, she sees herself sitting on a high bridge over a body of water with an image of God beside her. "I sort out the garbage—the worry, anxiety, unfinished business—and I throw it in the water. I feel a great relief by putting it somewhere else." At other times, Flora calls to mind an image of a shining light. "I shine it on the problem or on the person I am having trouble with. I can see the person revived or changing expression."

Nancy Seeks Spiritual Growth

Nancy prays on a daily basis, but occasionally she asks a friend to keep her children overnight so she can clear her mind and focus more intensely on her spiritual growth.

Odella Finds Peace in Walks

Odella goes walking when she needs quiet time. "When I walk near the lake and into the woods, I can immediately get into a very quiet, peaceful place within myself where I imagine myself going to think. I tell people I cannot talk to anybody until I talk to myself and know what my head is telling me. Once, I was so upset and confused I couldn't pray. I remember deciding I would have to use my confusion as a prayer, and I remember feeling real good about that."

We can pray or meditate in any form, anywhere, any time, for any length of time. Many books, classes, and counselors offer excellent suggestions to help us. If we are new at this, or if we need to find new ways to do it, it may take us a little time to feel at home with daily prayer and meditation. We can try several approaches until we find what works best to bring us into closer contact with our Higher Power. At first, a minute or two may be all we can manage comfortably. Gradually, we can increase these daily periods to ten or twenty minutes or more. We need not concern ourselves with how perfectly we do this. If we simply ask to know the will of God and for the power to carry that out, we can proceed with confidence, knowing we will be given what we need at every moment.

EXERCISE: A MEDITATION METHOD

Here is a guide for one type of meditation.

Sit in a comfortable position or lie down. Close your eyes. Take several deep breaths to relax yourself. As your breathing returns to normal, take notice of your breath going in and out. As you exhale, breathe out anxiety, tiredness, fear. As you inhale, breathe in love, harmony, joy. After doing this several times, you will relax more deeply. Create in your mind a beautiful, warm, quiet place and imagine yourself being there. Feel in your body the relaxation and joy of being in this place. Imagine the comfort of finding your Higher Power there beside you. Tell your Higher Power how you are feeling about being there. Express your gratitude for all you have received. Ask with humility to know God's will. Then gently dismiss any passing chatter in your mind and listen quietly for a time. You will receive guidance. Accept whatever comes, whether words, images, or a sense of reassurance, or just the quiet moment of being with God. Know that whatever comes, it is enough for today. Express your gratitude again. When you are ready, return your mind to the place where you began the meditation. Slowly open your eyes, and move on with your day in peace.

EXERCISE: AFFIRMING OURSELVES

One purpose for prayer and meditation is to open your heart and mind to new, God-directed ways of thinking. Our ordinary mind chatter is filled with many "old tapes," messages we heard over and over again earlier in our life, especially in childhood. Many of these are unhealthy messages, such as "Always put others first," "Don't take chances," or "Never get angry."

We can use our time of prayer and meditation to replace those messages with more positive ones. We can say affirmations. Affirmations are short, positive statements in the present tense that plant firmly in our mind and heart the reality we want for ourselves. Affirmations are most helpful if they are repeated frequently, with conviction. Many people write them out and carry them in their wallets or purses; some post them at home and at work where they see them often as reminders during the day.

Here are a few suggested affirmations:

- I am relaxed and at peace.
- I am an energetic, healthy, and creative person.
- I live in harmony with God's will.
- I enjoy my work and do it effortlessly.
- God's love guides me at all times.
- I exercise daily.
- I honor my emotions and express them in healthy ways.
- I surrender control to my Higher Power.

You can create affirmations of your own. Whatever affirmations you use, repeat them often. Ask your Higher Power for guidance. Gradually, these affirmations will help make your image of yourself and your world more positive. Your self-talk will change, and so will your actions. Chances are you will achieve your desires more easily and quickly.

> STEP TWELVE: Having had a spiritual awakening as the result of these steps, we tried to carry this message to other caregivers, and to practice these principles in all our affairs.

In a way, most of us were asleep before we encountered the Twelve Steps. We were asleep to the heavy toll our obsession with our caregiving responsibilities was taking on us. We were asleep to how many of our beliefs and behaviors were getting in our way. We were asleep to the spiritual resources within and around us.

The first eleven Steps have been a wake-up call. Now, we are alert to things we could not or would not see before. We have actively surrendered our unmanageable life to our Higher Power, cleared up our past misdeeds, and equipped ourselves with daily supports to live a saner life. We have had a spiritual awakening.

We Have Changed

Because of that awakening, we have changed and our life has changed. We may be unable to put our finger on exactly what has made the difference, but both in quiet times and crises, we operate with a fresh outlook. We are more aware of our own feelings and needs, and we respect them. For the most part, we neither try to play God with others nor let anyone lord over us. A growing self-esteem puts us on a more equal footing with all. We are less preoccupied with worries about the future or regrets over the past, preferring instead to live One Day at a Time. The rest we leave in our Higher Power's hands.

We may still feel frustrated because of our powerlessness over the condition of our loved one. We may still have some feelings of guilt over not doing enough or not doing the right thing. We may still resent the actions of others and feel sorry for ourselves at times. But we are now able to rebound from these and other painful moments more quickly. As one woman put it, "I am getting toppled over all the time, but I climb back into the boat."

Instead of being harsh with ourselves, we give ourselves love and acceptance. We can tell ourselves: *You happen to be human, and that's got to be enough for today.*

Having spent enormous energy exploring all the options available for the person we care for, we now also seek options for ourselves. Some of us found ways to take breaks from caregiving and to take up activities we enjoy. The Twelve Steps have given Marlene the freedom to leave her husband alone in the house for a couple of hours when she wants to go shopping or meet friends for lunch. "I feed him, I get him to the bathroom, and then I go. I don't think about him at all while I'm gone. If he falls, I don't have any guilt. He has a phone to call an emergency number. I know I can't control everything that happens."

Some of us became free to change our role substantially, for example, by involving other family members more actively in the caregiving or by moving the invalid out of our home into a different setting.

Some Difficult Decisions

Nancy's brain-injured husband had become a stranger to her. After his belligerent actions threatened the physical and emotional well-being of her and her children, she found a good place for him to live and receive the ongoing professional care he needed. After much soul-searching, she then decided on divorce. "I always thought I could fix anything. But I finally had to accept the fact that I couldn't do anything to change his condition, and it wasn't my responsibility to do so. I felt I did my best, I gave all I could, and it didn't work. I felt my sanity slipping away. I turned my decision over to my Higher Power, and my Higher Power helped me with it. I feel I made a good decision, and I have never regretted it."

Our spiritual awakening has these very practical applications. As caregivers, we have to make many tough decisions. The Twelve Steps give us a framework in which to make our decisions, and the ability to surrender outcomes to our Higher Power.

Sharing the Program

That's what Step Twelve offers us—an invitation to pass along the Twelve Step program to other caregivers. Our heart goes out to those who are still tangled up in the emotional disturbances of caregiving—we know how disheartened *we* were feeling before we were introduced to this program.

Finding other caregivers and sharing our experience, strength, and hope is our mission in Step Twelve. We do not have to look far. We can find caregivers—those caring for someone with a chronic condition—among our friends and relatives, in our church, in our neighborhood, at our work-place, and at the places where our loved one receives various services. Sharing our personal story will not only help others, but it will help us deepen our own program.

Rather than becoming an overzealous evangelist on behalf of the Twelve Steps, we may plant a seed by telling our story to another. We can trust that the other person has a Higher Power as a guide, just as we have. As others witness our ability to maintain serenity in trying circumstances, they will be attracted to us and will want to learn our secret. We gladly respond, but we avoid offering advice. What we can do, in addition to revealing our personal experience, is to share Twelve Step literature and other resources with them and to lend them an understanding ear. Ultimately, though, we allow others to be guided by their own Twelve Step experience.

Support Groups

Some days we ourselves need encouragement from others who understand. Self-help groups are a wonderful way to connect with other caregivers. These groups meet regularly to offer mutual support. Though it may be hard to find a self-help group for caregivers that focuses exclusively on the Twelve Steps, we can still learn a great deal from others in more general support groups for caregivers. Attending meetings of a support group also gives us opportunities to talk with others about our difficulties and our progress.

Most of us who practice the Twelve Steps, however, avoid giving advice or depending heavily on the advice of other caregivers for our own situation. We learn what we can from their experience, but we rely on our Higher Power and practice the Steps for ourselves.

Some caregivers find it helpful to attend meetings of other Twelve Step groups such as Al-Anon (for families of alco-holics), Adult Children of Alcoholics, Overeaters Anonymous, or Emotions Anonymous. Although our particular problem may be distinct from the focus of these groups, we have a similar pattern of being preoccupied with someone or something outside ourselves. We can use what we find helpful in these groups and leave the rest. Some caregivers have gathered together in Twelve Step groups that focus specifically on the concerns of caregiving. These groups hold meetings similar to those of other Twelve Step groups. Some of these caregiver groups are called Caregivers Anonymous.

Whatever the format, we find that giving and sharing support enriches our life. We become stronger as we experience a bond of understanding with other human beings. Our self-esteem grows and our worries diminish.

A Program for Life

Our Twelve Step program is a daily program. Steps Ten and Eleven give us checkpoints for charting our progress. Step Twelve asks caregivers to go even further, to practice these principles in *all* our affairs. Isn't that asking a lot? It is, but the secret to the success of this program is that it is not a short-term fix-it course, but a way of life. When we let it infiltrate our every action, we come to experience a deep confidence in ourselves and in our Higher Power. We trust in our Higher Power's wisdom to guide us over both the bumpy and the easy trails. We know a deep joy.

Joy and serenity transform our dark moments. Some such moments are accepted and passed through more quickly. Others are taken away. Some are even seen for what they are—gifts from God to lead us where we need to go. The Twelve Steps help us give up the illusion of perfection as defined by our ego. We now know that God's will is wiser, even when we can't see the wisdom in some situations.

An important skill caregivers have learned from the Twelve Steps is to set boundaries. We say no without feeling guilty.

We refuse to be responsible for someone else's behavior. In other words, we expect the people we care for and others in our life to manage their responsibilities to the level they are able. If they don't, we refrain from stepping in to rescue them. We also take care of our responsibilities, not expecting others to rescue us. We give out of love rather than duty or guilt. We speak honestly with everyone, respectfully letting others know what we like and want, as well as what we will not accept from them.

At times, the boundaries are not so easy to set. If the person we care for is in the hospital in critical condition, how long should we stay by the person's side? If we have been there for eighteen hours, is that long enough? Can we go home for a while? Or should we never leave the hospital until the crisis is passed? Where do we draw the line? When does our need for rest and relaxation take priority over the other person's life-and-death struggles? When do we give our all? No set answers exist for these and many other dilemmas we face. We have only our Higher Power to guide us. We pray, make our decisions, and trust that all will be well.

Some days, too, everything feels devastating. We feel weak, scared, and tired. Sometimes we say the Serenity Prayer all day long. Admittedly, there are even days when we lose our self-control. We go to pieces. But through the support of others in the program, through the literature, or through some other gift from our Higher Power, we are renewed. We find hope again, and we go on.

> *The Larsens: Throughout our years of active caregiving, the two of us called on all the resources the Twelve Step program has to offer. We still do, because we find the Twelve Step principles apply to all our affairs, and also because we still find ourselves in the role of caregiver from time to time. In fact, as we each face various health*

challenges ourselves, we occasionally become caregivers for one another.

Thus, as we did when Beth and Frances were in our care, we cherish our weekly meetings with a group of couples who practice the Twelve Steps, we are faithful to our morning inventory, and we try our best to remember to look to God throughout each day. We are grateful that during Beth's final years this program helped us on a daily basis to mourn the loss of her active presence and eventually to mourn the death of both Frances and Beth. It gave us a way to find peace of mind in challenging circumstances one day at a time, and it still does.

A special time of peace came just after our friend, Frances, died. She had asked that we remember her with a celebration rather than a funeral. With balloons of yellow and green (her favorite colors) as decorations, we gathered in our living room with the friends who knew Frances to pay tribute to her in songs, stories, and prayer. As she had requested, guests brought seeds and small plants, and we have planted a garden in our backyard that will help her live long in our memory. Frances's garden also reminds us again and again of the peace that continues to grow within us.

That peace is the ultimate gift of the Twelve Steps for all of us caregivers.

EXERCISE: A GAME FOR LIFE

There is a game called "Snake" that children play. A group of children, preferably a large group, holds hands in a line. The leader, at the head of the "snake," begins running and all the children are pulled along. As the leader goes faster and faster and weaves back and forth, the child at the snake's tail, of course, is whipped about.

In the child's game, this is all in good fun. But sometimes, caregivers feel a little like that child at the end of the snake, snapped around mercilessly by circumstances. And it's not much fun. We feel that our only hope is to hang on for dear life.

Imagine yourself for a moment at the snake's tail. (This shouldn't be hard if you've recently had a rough day.) Is your only option to be swung about out of control?

What if you looked for another snake, and with your free hand, grasped the free hand of its "head" (the leader), joining the two snakes and putting you in an easier-flowing, center-of-the-line position?

Or what if you spotted a place for a soft landing and let go of the hand that was holding yours?

What if, in a moment when you were weaving around, you came close enough to the head of your snake to grab that person's free hand? Then imagine forming a circle and perhaps initiating a less risky game.

What if you hung on tight, went "with the flow," and laughed like a child?

What if you yelled "Stop!" at the top of your lungs?

Consider how the Twelve Steps can help you deal with the occasions where you routinely feel powerless in your daily life. How can you find the support you need? In what situations would you do well to yell "Stop!"? Which ones could you surrender to and laugh about because they can't be changed?

Conclusion

Our goal in writing this book is to offer hope. If, within its pages, you have seen some possibility for greater meaning and peace of mind, please continue to push open the door of possibility a little further. Admittedly, some of its ideas may have puzzled you a bit. Others may seem out of reach. You may have objections or at least hesitations about some. These reactions are perfectly normal. It is not important to understand or accept everything you have read at once. The Twelve Steps are not a bunch of hard and fast rules. Rather, they outline a spiritual approach to living. If you found something within them that appeals to you, start with that. Begin in a way that feels comfortable for you. Write about it, pray about it, talk to someone you trust. Use whatever means you find helpful to explore the Twelve Step path, a little at a time. You will find the guidance you need as you go. The following slogans, commonly used in the program, can assist you.

Keep It Simple

One of the slogans of the Twelve Step program is Keep It Simple. And that's especially wise at first. This is not a complicated program. Rather, it is about accepting what is real and being honest and loving in our day-to-day living. The Steps are there to guide us. The stories and support of others give it concrete expression. Then we make it our own, learning to trust the guidance that ultimately comes from deep within ourselves.

One Day at a Time

We've already learned that we can live this program only One Day at a Time—another Twelve Step slogan. By keeping that in mind, we avoid worrying about what the future might bring or becoming swallowed up in resentments or regrets about the past. Each day, each moment, we have everything we need to meet what lies before us. As caregivers, there will be moments when we feel that all we can do is to hold on moment by moment. Living the Twelve Steps, we eventually become able to surrender to what comes each moment, knowing that it is our Higher Power's will for us. Once we know that all we have to live through is the very moment we are in, we are free to be fully alive in that moment.

Easy Does It

Another slogan is Easy Does It. That's an important reminder for caregivers. We tend to work hard, push hard, try hard, and be hard on ourselves. Easy Does It helps us to remember to take things a little easier. We can trust that all will be well, whether or not we are in control or have all the answers. Moderation is a good guide. We do what we can, and leave the rest to our Higher Power. We are not responsible for the outcome, only for the effort. Even the effort may be difficult to make some days, and we can again rely on our Higher Power to do what we cannot.

This Too Shall Pass

Crises come time and time again. We feel scared, lonely, angry, hurt, sad, disappointed, even desperately bored. But in time, everything passes. Neither our panic and frantic activity nor our running and hiding do much to change what happens. Trust, love, and forgiveness serve us better. Through this program, we learn that everything happens for a reason. We look to find the gift for ourselves in every event and person we encounter. We become grateful that serenity is always available. We have only to accept it, moment by moment.

Let Go and Let God

Ultimately, Let Go and Let God is the message that reassures us that someone else is in charge, and we don't have to be. We say the Serenity Prayer and release our every concern, knowing an all-loving power is wiser than we are. We find peace in that. We relax. We let go.

May you find the peace within that passes all understanding.

Appendix One

THE TWELVE STEPS OF ALCOHOLICS ANONYMOUS*

1. We admitted we were powerless over alcohol—that our lives had become unmanageable.

2. Came to believe that a Power greater than ourselves could restore us to sanity.

3. Made a decision to turn our will and our lives over to the care of God *as we understood Him.*

4. Made a searching and fearless moral inventory of ourselves.

5. Admitted to God, to ourselves, and to another human being the exact nature of our wrongs.

6. Were entirely ready to have God remove all these defects of character.

7. Humbly asked Him to remove our shortcomings.

8. Made a list of all persons we had harmed, and became willing to make amends to them all.

9. Made direct amends to such people wherever possible, except when to do so would injure them or others.

10. Continued to take personal inventory and when we were wrong promptly admitted it.

11. Sought through prayer and meditation to improve our conscious contact with God *as we understood Him,* praying only for knowledge of His will for us and the power to carry that out.

12. Having had a spiritual awakening as the result of these steps, we tried to carry this message to alcoholics, and to practice these principles in all our affairs.

*The Twelve Steps of AA are taken from *Alcoholics Anonymous*, 3d ed., published by AA World Services, Inc., New York, N.Y., 59–60. Reprinted with permission of AA World Services, Inc.

Appendix Two

THE TWELVE STEPS FOR CAREGIVERS*

1. We admitted we were powerless over the people we are taking care of—that our lives had become unmanageable.

2. Came to believe that a Power greater than ourselves could restore us to sanity.

3. Made a decision to turn our will and our lives over to the care of God *as we understood God.*

4. Made a searching and fearless moral inventory of ourselves.

5. Admitted to God, to ourselves, and to another human being the exact nature of our wrongs.

6. Were entirely ready to have God remove all these defects of character.

7. Humbly asked God to remove our shortcomings.

8. Made a list of all persons we had harmed, and became willing to make amends to them all.

9. Made direct amends to such people wherever possible, except when to do so would injure them or others.

10. Continued to take personal inventory and when we were wrong promptly admitted it.

11. Sought through prayer and meditation to improve our conscious contact with God *as we understood God,* praying only for knowledge of God's will for us and the power to carry that out.

12. Having had a spiritual awakening as the result of these steps, we tried to carry this message to other caregivers, and to practice these principles in all our affairs.

*The Twelve Steps for Caregivers are adapted from the Twelve Steps of Alcoholics Anonymous. Reprinted with permission of AA World Services, Inc.

Hazelden Foundation, a national nonprofit organization founded in 1949, helps people reclaim their lives from the disease of addiction. Built on decades of knowledge and experience, Hazelden's comprehensive approach to addiction addresses the full range of individual, family, and professional needs, including addiction treatment and continuing care services for youth and adults, publishing, research, higher learning, public education, and advocacy.

A life of recovery is lived "one day at a time." Hazelden publications, both educational and inspirational, support and strengthen lifelong recovery. In 1954, Hazelden published *Twenty-Four Hours a Day,* the first daily meditation book for recovering alcoholics, and Hazelden continues to publish works to inspire and guide individuals in treatment and recovery, and their loved ones. Professionals who work to prevent and treat addiction also turn to Hazelden for evidence-based curricula, informational materials, and videos for use in schools, treatment programs, and correctional programs.

Through published works, Hazelden extends the reach of hope, encouragement, help, and support to individuals, families, and communities affected by addiction and related issues.

For questions about Hazelden publications, please call **800-328-9000** or visit us online at **hazelden.org/bookstore.**

Bibliography

Alcoholics Anonymous, 3d ed. New York: AA World Services, Inc., 1976.

Carter, Rosalynn, and Susan K. Golant. *Helping Yourself Help Others: A Book for Caregivers.* New York: Times Books, 1996.

Cleveland, Martha. *Chronic Illness and the Twelve Steps: A Practical Approach to Spiritual Resilience.* Center City, Minn.: Hazelden, 1988.

Klaas, Joe. *The 12 Steps to Happiness.* New York: Ballantine Books, 1993.

Kushner, Harold S. *When Bad Things Happen to Good People.* New York: Harper Collins, 1994.

McLeod, Beth Witrogen. *Caregiving: The Spirtual Journey of Love, Loss, and Renewal.* New York: John Wiley & Sons, 1999.

Strong, Maggie. *Mainstay: For the Well Spouse of the Chronically Ill.* N.p.: Bradford Books, 1997.

Twelve Steps and Twelve Traditions. New York: AA World Services, Inc., 1976.

About the Authors:

Pat Samples is a writer and transformational educator. Her five other books include *Daily Comforts for Caregivers* and *The Twelve Steps and Dual Disorders*. She edits *The Phoenix,* a newspaper for people in Twelve Step recovery programs. Samples also speaks and gives workshops on self-care to family and professional caregivers and on other personal developement topics. She lives in Brooklyn Center, Minnesota, a suburb of Minneapolis, and is actively involved in Twelve Step programs.

Involved in Twelve Step work for more than a decade, Diane and Marvin Larsen have been primary caregivers for three friends and relatives. Most recently, they cared for Diane's mother, who had Alzheimer's disease. They live in Gaylord, Minnesota.